SPIRITUAL BUT NOT RELIGIOUS

Spiritual But Not Religious: The Basics is an accessible guide to the defining attributes of individuals who define themselves as Spiritual but Not Religious (SBNR), who comprise at least 25% of the American population. Topics covered include:

- What does it mean to consider oneself "religious" or "spiritual"?
- What historical or cultural forces have prompted people to distinguish between them and identify as "spiritual" but not "religious"?
- How did today's expressions of SBNR emerge?
- What are SBNR beliefs/practices?
- What are the criticisms of SBNR posed both by those who are nonreligious and those who are more conventionally religious?
- What is the future of SBNR in economically developed nations?

The book introduces the broad spectrum of beliefs and practices associated with individuals who identify as being spiritual but not religious. Featuring portraits of real people's experiences of being SBNR, the book explains the terminology, historical background, contemporary expressions, and probable future of this enduring strain of American religiosity. This is the go-to resource for anyone interested in understanding more about the beliefs of those who are spiritual but not religious.

Robert C. Fuller is Distinguished University Professor of Religious Studies, Emeritus at Bradley University, USA.

William B. Parsons is the Harry and Hazel Chavanne Professor in Christianity and Director of the graduate program in religion at Rice University, USA.

The Basics

THOMAS AQUINAS
FRANKLIN T. HARKINS

BIBLE AND FILM
MATTHEW S. RINDGE

RELIGION AND FILM
JEANETTE REEDY SOLANO

SECULARISM
JACQUES BERLINERBLAU

FILM MUSIC
KENNETH LAMPL

JEWISH ETHICS
GEOFFREY D. CLAUSSEN

QUAKERISM (SECOND EDITION)
MARGERY POST ABBOTT AND CARL ABBOTT

SIKHISM
NIKKY-GUNINDER KAUR SINGH AND ELEANOR NESBITT

ORTHODOX CHRISTIANITY
NICHOLAS E. DENYSENKO

FEMINIST THEOLOGIES
SUSAN M. SHAW AND GRACE JI-SUN KIM

QUEER THEOLOGIES (SECOND EDITION)
CHRIS GREENOUGH

PHILOSOPHICAL THEOLOGY
DAFYDD MILLS DANIEL AND DAVID MILLS DANIEL

NEW RELIGIOUS MOVEMENTS (SECOND EDITION)
JOSEPH P. LAYCOCK

SPIRITUAL BUT NOT RELIGIOUS
ROBERT C. FULLER AND WILLIAM B. PARSONS

For more information about this series, please visit: https://www.routledge.com/The-Basics/book-series/B

SPIRITUAL BUT NOT RELIGIOUS

THE BASICS

Robert C. Fuller
and William B. Parsons

LONDON AND NEW YORK

Designed cover image: Cinefootage Visuals via Getty Images

First published 2027
by Routledge
4 Park Square, Milton Park, Abingdon, Oxon OX14 4RN

and by Routledge
605 Third Avenue, New York, NY 10158

Routledge is an imprint of the Taylor & Francis Group, an informa business

© 2027 Robert C. Fuller and William B. Parsons

The right of Robert C. Fuller and William B. Parsons to be identified as authors of this work has been asserted in accordance with sections 77 and 78 of the Copyright, Designs and Patents Act 1988.

All rights reserved. No part of this book may be reprinted or reproduced or utilised in any form or by any electronic, mechanical, or other means, now known or hereafter invented, including photocopying and recording, or in any information storage or retrieval system, without permission in writing from the publishers.

For Product Safety Concerns and Information please contact our EU representative GPSR@taylorandfrancis.com. Taylor & Francis Verlag GmbH, Kaufingerstraße 24, 80331 München, Germany.

Trademark notice: Product or corporate names may be trademarks or registered trademarks, and are used only for identification and explanation without intent to infringe.

British Library Cataloguing-in-Publication Data
A catalogue record for this book is available from the British Library

Library of Congress Cataloging-in-Publication Data
Names: Fuller, Robert C., 1952- author | Parsons, William Barclay, 1955- author
Title: Spiritual but not religious : the basics / Robert C. Fuller
and William B. Parsons.
Other titles: Spiritual but not religious (Routledge (Firm))
Description: Abingdon, Oxon ; New York, NY : Routledge, 2027. |
Series: The basics | Includes bibliographical references and index. |
Identifiers: LCCN 2026012974 (print) | LCCN 2026012975 (ebook) |
ISBN 9781032994574 hardback | ISBN 9781032994567 paperback |
ISBN 9781003604259 ebook
Subjects: LCSH: Spirituality--North America--History | Spirituality--Europe--History |
North America--Religion | Europe, Western--Religion
Classification: LCC BL624 .F85 2027 (print) | LCC BL624 (ebook)
LC record available at https://lccn.loc.gov/2026012974
LC ebook record available at https://lccn.loc.gov/2026012975

ISBN: 9781032994574 (hbk)
ISBN: 9781032994567 (pbk)
ISBN: 9781003604259 (ebk)

DOI: 10.4324/9781003604259

Typeset in Sabon
by KnowledgeWorks Global Ltd.

CONTENTS

1 **Terms and definitions** 1

2 **SBNR's beginnings** 18

3 **Combining diverse perspectives** 41

4 **Being SBNR: beliefs, practices, personality profiles** 66

5 **Criticisms and debates** 93

6 **Glimpsing the future** 114

7 **Retracing our steps** 129

SBNR portraits 136
Appendix: for further reading 150
Index 161

1

TERMS AND DEFINITIONS

Individuals who describe themselves as "Spiritual but Not Religious" (SBNR) comprise somewhere from 22% to 27% of the American population. This percentage is significantly higher among those under 40. The percentage of Canadians who identify as SBNR is slightly higher. And although the percentage of SBNRs across all countries of Western Europe is only about 11%, it is much higher in Scandinavian nations and also among Europeans in their 20s and 30s. Being SBNR, then, is now an established outlook in modern Western nations. Its recent history and new expressions make for an interesting story. This story, as we will see, opens windows that allow us to gain fresh looks at many of the social, philosophical, and even psychological forces that shape modern life.

This book will examine the emergence and spread of the SBNR movement in both Western Europe and North America. We might remind ourselves that for almost two thousand years, Christianity has been the dominant religious tradition in the Western world. Being religious in Western nations has therefore centered around its doctrines, ritual practices, and cultural outlook. It is true that most people throughout history have, to some degree, privately fashioned their own religious outlook by selectively emphasizing some elements of religious faith and largely ignoring other elements. But relatively, few individuals have braved the social consequences of religious nonconformity by outwardly rejecting the group's prevailing belief system. The emergence of a widespread SBNR movement therefore required the freedom to choose for oneself, an

DOI: 10.4324/9781003604259-1

option not publicly condoned for much of history. The growth of personal freedoms in western, democratic countries made it possible for the early expressions of the SBNR movement to gain traction. Theocratic nations such as modern-day Iran discourage and even punish alternative ways of being religious. Totalitarian governments such as China discourage religion in general and especially newly emerging belief systems that encourage individual expression. What we today refer to as the SBNR movement is therefore primarily found in nations whose political and economic structures resemble those of the Western world. It might be noted that many features of the SBNR movement have been historically present in countries such as India and Japan—but their stories will lie outside the scope of this book. Both the words "spirituality" and "religion" are used very differently in countries like India or Japan and, hence, require far more cultural contextualization than this book can provide. This book, then, will largely focus on what it means to be spiritual but not religious, in modern Western societies.[1]

We used to think that there are two basic categories when it comes to religion—being religious or being nonreligious. The first and largest category consisted of people who were religious. Being religious meant publicly conforming to the doctrines, rituals, and lifestyle codes associated with a formal religious tradition. Being religious communicated a basic affirmation of a religious tradition's holy books, ordained officials, and moral teachings. The second category consisted of a much smaller group of people unaffiliated with any kind of religious organization. Many of the nonreligious adhered to a wholly rational outlook that excluded ideas or practices that were in any way associated with supernatural beliefs. A few of those belonging to this second category turned their back on religion owing to some kind of negative experience with existing religious authorities or teachings.

Over the past two generations, it has become increasingly clear that these two categories don't sufficiently account for the many forms of religiosity we find throughout the Western world. One out of every four or five people now rejects either of these two categories and selects the third option of being "spiritual but not religious." Being SBNR has become so popular that journalists, pollsters, and scholars alike have found that they need to include it as a third principal way of gauging a person's stance toward religion. Indeed, almost all surveys hoping to gather basic information about people ask them to select which of three basic categories (being religious in a traditional, church-centered way; being wholly nonreligious, or being SBNR) best describes them. Being SBNR has become so common that even dating sites often include it as an optional way of describing ourselves.

There are, then, a lot of people who identify with this third category. But what does "being spiritual but not religious" really mean? What do they mean when they call themselves "spiritual"? What do they mean by saying they are "not religious"? What are the people who identify with being SBNR trying to say about themselves? What are they agreeing with? What are they disagreeing with?

An initial way of describing what it means to be "spiritual but not religious" is negative: we can say what it is *not*. It does *not* refer to those who have definitively settled in a particular institutionally based religious tradition, are happy with its ethical teachings, and are consistent in observing its services and rituals. In other words, being SBNR refers to those who are so disillusioned with traditional institutional religion that they seek other venues to satisfy their spiritual needs. At the same time, being SBNR can also be described in a positive way. Being SBNR means believing that religious traditions often contain deep wisdom. To say "I'm spiritual but not religious" indicates that a person seeks religious wisdom without fully committing to what they deem to be the outer trappings of religion (i.e., dogma, rituals, authority structures, etc.). Using a consumer analogy, it speaks to those who shop around multiple religious traditions, selecting only those insights that best meet their individual needs.

Contemporary scholarship can tell us even more about what it means to be SBNR. Interviewing people who identify as SBNR shows, for example, that these individuals are suspicious of organized religion. They have observed how institutional religion has often been complicit in sustaining gender inequalities and structural racism. They have seen how institutional religion has, throughout history, functioned to perpetuate the political and economic advantages of the rich—at the expense of the lower classes, who are taught to be humble and obedient to authority. They have seen how often religion has opposed scientific discoveries in order to defend literal interpretations of ancient texts. Those who identify as being SBNR wish to distance themselves from the seeming backwardness of organized religion. In doing so, they emphasize individualism and free choice. They tend to favor social equality, progressivism, and forms of religiosity that serve the individual's personal growth rather than maintaining existing social structures. Those who embrace SBNR come from diverse educational, ethnic, and racial backgrounds and tend to lean center-left politically. They see humans as basically good (and reject notions of "original sin"). Yet, unlike those who opt for the category of being wholly nonreligious, those in the category of being SBNR are drawn to a variety of concepts that are overtly supernatural or metaphysical (e.g., the existence of nonvisible spiritual energies, auras, paranormal mental abilities, reincarnation).[2]

Being SBNR is about exploring and experimenting. As a result, there are as many combinations of beliefs/practices as there are people who adopt this stance toward religiosity. Hollywood has given us a few stereotypes of what being SBNR might look like, such as the disillusioned character played by Laura Dern in the HBO series *Enlightened*. Dern's character spends 50 thousand dollars to go to a New Age retreat center in Hawaii, where she meditates, practices yoga, and undergoes therapy en route to achieving some kind of spiritual enlightenment (and then returns home, where she energetically tries to change her friends, family, and coworkers). In another hit TV show, *Mad Men*, a stressed-out advertising executive finds respite at the famous California institute known as Esalen. Attending lectures, participating in workshops, and practicing meditation help him let go of material striving and find an inner connection with a higher reality. Amusingly, the spiritually energized advertising executive was inspired to come up with a new advertising jingle ("I'd like to buy the world a coke")—a jingle that, in real life, was recorded by a group known as the New Seekers, the underlying meaning of the lyrics being to bring love and harmony to all the inhabitants of the Earth.

These are, of course, only media stereotypes of how actual people piece together a personal belief system that somehow exists in the "no-man's land" lying between church-centered religiosity and a total rejection of all forms of religion. We should keep in mind that many people who start picking and choosing their own beliefs and practices might actually continue to affiliate with a church, temple, or synagogue. They just no longer feel bound by this affiliation. They simply filter out or ignore whatever doesn't seem to further them on their own spiritual journey. For them, being SBNR sometimes shades into being "spiritual and religious."

Being SBNR is thus no single thing. What applies to some individuals and their journeys won't apply to others. But we can identify certain broad patterns. The aim of *Spiritual But Not Religious: The Basics* is to do precisely this: to identify the recurring themes and shared attitudes that define this admittedly amorphous "third category" of modern religious life.

THE TERMS "SPIRITUALITY" AND "RELIGION"

All of us have some idea about what the word "religion" means. What probably comes to mind first when we think about religion is that it entails belief: belief in a god, belief in an afterlife, belief in divine revelation or holy books, etc. We also think about religious practices: praying, attending worship services, confessing sins, singing hymns, celebrating sacred holidays, engaging in a pilgrimage, fasting, etc. And, too, we think of formal religious traditions or organizations: Christianity, Judaism, Islam, Buddhism, Hinduism, etc. It is, however, very difficult to define the word "religion" precisely. What distinguishes being religious from all other domains of human existence such as political, social, cultural, or economic?

Academic scholars have debated the definition of "religion" for decades. They point out that not every religion believes in gods or supernatural beings. Nor does every religion hold beliefs about an afterlife. What does seem to characterize the various cultural expressions we designate as "religion" is belief in the existence of some more-than-physical reality. That is, what separates religion from other domains of human existence is the underlying belief that there is "more" to the universe than can be detected with the five physical senses. What further separates religion from other domains is religion's belief that humans will find their highest fulfillment only by aligning themselves with this more-than-physical dimension of the universe. The psychologist and philosopher William James summarized the core meaning of the term "religion" when he wrote that being religious stems from "the belief that there is an unseen order, and that our supreme good lies in harmoniously adjusting ourselves thereto."[3] Throughout history, then, humans have believed that there is more to the universe than can be detected by our physical senses or by the scientific method. This book is about those who share this belief, but explore these "unseen orders" and experiment with techniques that might "harmoniously adjust themselves thereto" outside established religious organizations.

Every human society has had some form of religious belief and some form of religious ritual. And, too, almost every human society has recognized certain individuals who appear particularly adept at explaining this "unseen order" and prescribing methods whereby individuals might harmoniously adjust themselves thereto. At some point, these explanations and methods give rise to enduring institutions that perpetuate very specific doctrines, rituals, scriptures, bureaucratic hierarchies, and places of worship—in short, organized religion. And thus, "being religious" in any given human society has almost always meant embracing and conforming to the teachings and methods of organized religion.

What, then, about the word "spiritual"? In the Christian New Testament, St. Paul refers to *spiritus* as a term he used to signify those individuals whose mind, will, and heart were ordered and led by the "spirit" (over against those egoistically attached to and led by the things of the world). For most of Western cultural history, being spiritual meant ordering one's life in accordance with church teachings. At one point, the term was actually used in a juridical sense to denote ecclesiastical offices and property.

It is important to note the close connection between the term "spirituality" and what we refer to as mysticism. The two terms are, in fact, often used interchangeably. The term "mysticism" can be traced back to the ancient Greek mystery religions. At first, *mystikos* referred only to the hidden or secret elements of ritualistic activities and didn't specifically refer to any transcendent or "unseen" dimension of reality. The term was later picked up by the early Church Fathers. The Church Fathers were drawing attention to the fact that their contemplative practices brought one into contact with the God of Christianity. In their view, contemplative practices could only lead to genuine mystical experiences of God when accessed through the auspices of church and tradition. These early Christian leaders taught that mystical contemplation leads to experiences of a "Reality" above and beyond any other kind of human sensation. As Louis Boyer explains, in early Christianity, mysticism was thought to be "the experience of an invisible objective world: the world whose coming the Scriptures reveal to us in Jesus Christ, the world into which we enter, ontologically, through the liturgy."[4]

As time went on, however, the meanings of both mystical experience and spirituality began to shift in ways that sound more contemporary and unchurched. This trend started in the sixteenth and seventeenth centuries, when even those who pursued mystical experiences within Christian monasteries increasingly employed language that was highly individualistic and focused on subjective feelings or sensations. In this sense, spirituality was a more solitary pursuit and, to some extent, divorced from church and tradition. The Christian mystics of this era increasingly moved away from biblical terminology about a supreme human-like being when they wrote about their experiences of God. Indeed, those who wrote about mystical experience frequently depicted the divine in impersonal terminology, often replacing images of a heavenly father with more generic terms such as "the Absolute." Those Christians drawn to the mystic often depicted the divine as a reality hidden beneath a diversity of theological institutions, religious structures, and doctrines. The implication was that an authentic mystical or spiritual experience somehow brings individuals into direct contact with a divine order that is itself unmediated by any worldly institution.

This historical shift from viewing spirituality in institutional contexts to wholly individual contexts is vividly demonstrated in William James' masterpiece, *The Varieties of Religious Experience*. James was himself the recipient of mystical insights. But his mystical experiences occurred when immersed in nature or during drug-induced (nitrous oxide) altered states of consciousness. They had taken place wholly outside of organized religion. It is thus not surprising that James framed mysticism in a way diametrically opposed to that found in the early Church Fathers. James proclaimed that most of what we associate with religion (its doctrines, rituals, and institutions) is only second-hand religion. First-hand, authentic religion arises in personal experience, which he describes as "the feelings, acts and experiences of individual[s] in their solitude, so far as they apprehend themselves to stand in relation to whatever they may consider the divine."[5] James identified the primary characteristics of a genuine mystical experience as passivity, ineffability, transiency, and unity. All of these pertain to characteristics of personal experience rather than articles of Christian theology. James believed that mystical experiences were the primary data or core of authentic religion. Everything else, including theology, liturgy, ritual, and the various aspects of church organizations were said to be secondary phenomenon. James was thus proclaiming that authentic religiosity grew from private, personal experience rather than participation in organized religion.

The publication of James's book in 1902 was both a cause and a symptom of a real shift happening in Western culture. The early Church Fathers viewed the institutional church to be essential for gaining access to the "presence of God." But by 1902, a large segment of Western society no longer turned to organized religion for insights into a higher or "unseen order." Nor did they consider religious institutions particularly helpful in showing us the lifestyles or practices through which we might best adjust ourselves harmoniously thereto.

It was now thought possible to undertake one's own spiritual journey independently of church authorities. Spirituality had been cut loose from its former institutional moorings and was now understood in the wider cultural frameworks of democratization and individualization.

THE TERM "SPIRITUAL BUT NOT RELIGIOUS"

We can pinpoint the first historical use of the term "spiritual but not religious." It first appeared in 1926 when the president of the Rotary Club described his organization as inclusive, nonsectarian, and as SBNR.[6] Even this early use of the phrase contains several characteristics that many associate with being SBNR even today (i.e., nontraditional or "unchurched," inclusive and nonsectarian, affiliated with free-market rather than controlled socio-economic systems). It is hard to know exactly what either the author of this Rotary Club article or its readers understood by the terms "religious" or "spiritual." It is probable that most of those who read this article belonged to one or another of the culturally dominant Protestant denominations of the day (e.g., Presbyterians, Congregationalists, Episcopalians). Members of these denominations would probably have some general knowledge about any number of liberal religious traditions (e.g., Transcendentalists, Unitarians, Quakers) and their advocacy of a wide range of cultural values: individuality, solitude, inner silence and meditation, ethical reforms, and creative self-expression. Most had probably read at least a few of the essays written by such highly regarded American writers as Ralph Waldo Emerson, Walt Whitman, Henry David Thoreau, or Margaret Fuller. All of these progressive voices encouraged individuals to undertake their own personal journeys toward what Walt Whitman described as the "spirituality of religion," which was thought to arise only from "perfect uncontamination" and "solitariness of individuality." The Rotary Club president was thus not writing in a cultural vacuum. He and his audience were fully aware of strong cultural currents that were pulling citizens of Western nations toward an unchurched, nontraditional, even anti-institutional orientation towards the divine.[7]

This Rotary Club article may be the earliest publication that uses the phrase "spiritual but not religious," but it didn't play any role in putting this phrase into our modern vocabulary. It only appeared in the club's internal newsletter, *The American Mercury*, and was probably only read by a hundred people or so. The person who most successfully popularized the phrase is undoubtedly the founder of Alcoholics Anonymous, Bill Wilson. Bill Wilson (or simply Bill W., as he is known within the movement) was himself an alcoholic who became acutely aware of his inability to overcome his addiction. Finally, in a moment of desperation, Bill W. found himself crying out, "If there is a God, let Him show Himself! I am ready to do anything, anything."

Suddenly the room lit up with a great white light. I was caught up into an ecstasy which there are no words to describe.... All about me and through me there was a wonderful feeling of Presence, and I thought to myself, "So this is the God of the preachers!" A great peace stole over me and I thought, "No matter how wrong things seem to be, they are all right. Things are all right with God and His world."[8]

This experience became the paradigm of self-renewal for Alcoholics Anonymous. What is striking about this passage, too, is how it voices many of SBNR's central themes. His references to God shift from envisioning a male Supreme Being to conceptualizing God as an impersonal presence, light, or energetic power. He depicts personal renewal as an automatic consequence of letting go of one's normal ego-centered rationality. The receptive self then became inwardly receptive to a great white light or a Presence. And all of this transpired without any reliance on religious clergy, institutional sacraments, or dependence on scriptural authority. Bill W. was, in fact, extremely skeptical of organized religion. He was especially suspicious of the moralism associated with religious institutions. Most alcoholics had endured more than their share of pious admonitions to cease sinning. He rejected traditional religious dogma and confessed that "in all probability, the churches will not supply the answers for a good many of us."[9]

There are a few other ways that Bill W. played a pivotal role in the origins of the modern SBNR movement. One such way was that he immersed himself in the insights of two spiritually oriented psychologists, Carl Jung and William James. The Swiss psychoanalyst Carl Jung had treated Rowland H., another pioneer of Alcoholics Anonymous. Jung believed that alcoholics suffered from personality conflicts so profound as to be incurable through conventional scientific methods. He deemed that such dramatic transformations resulted from experiences that are deeply spiritual in nature. Jung, too, had struggled with organized religion. Although his father was a Lutheran minister, he ultimately rejected Christian doctrines because he believed they no longer spoke to the modern individual. Jung instead came to speak of God as "the collective unconscious," a source of healing power available to everyone at the depths of their minds or consciousness. It was from Jung that Alcoholics Anonymous borrowed ways of explaining why the rational self must first give way before the regenerative process can begin. Jung's argument was psychological rather than theological. For him, it was simply the case that the waking personality is too rationalistic and egocentric to permit higher influences to enter. Alcoholics Anonymous's insistence on "letting go to a Higher Power" was therefore not motivated by conventional religion's belief in human depravity. It was, instead, based on psychological principles. Alcoholics who finally gave up control of their lives to a higher power (residing deep within themselves) experienced what Bill W. had described as an ecstasy and a wonderful feeling of Presence. Very few who attended Alcoholics Anonymous meetings or practiced its 12-step programs have ever read any of Carl Jung's publications. But they came away with at least some working knowledge of Jung's spiritually oriented psychology.

Even more important was the way that Bill W. paraphrased the thought of the American philosopher-psychologist William James. Bill W. came upon James's monumental *The Varieties of Religious Experience* shortly after his own recovery. James's psychological—rather than theological—explanation of religious experience emboldened Bill W. to abandon belief in the Bible or church teachings. He concurred with James's thesis that the "truth" of religion is to be found in personal experiences of a higher power. James maintained that all religious beliefs must be held tentatively and continuously revised as dictated by new knowledge or experience. He urged readers to adopt an open-minded, experimental approach to their spiritual journeys. He embraced religious diversity and celebrated (rather than condemned) the reasons why there are so many cultural and personal differences in this area of human life. When Bill W. once stated that William James was a "founder of Alcoholics Anonymous," he was only partially joking. For it was James who gave the movement a metaphysical vocabulary to explain its unique kind of spirituality that was at once deeply personal, optimistic, and couched in the language of self-actualization.

Bill W. worked tirelessly to introduce Alcoholics Anonymous to the American public. He did so by proclaiming it to be "a spiritual rather than a religious program."[10] And, in doing so, he injected this phrase into our everyday vernacular. Over the years, Alcoholics Anonymous toned down its metaphysical overtones and its criticism of Christian churches so that it wouldn't alienate larger audiences. It has nonetheless retained its distinctively spiritual flavor. The group's self-help manual *Twelve Steps and Twelve Traditions* continues to warn against relying on willpower or one's own personal resources. It counsels that the path toward personal renewal requires attaining "the feeling of being at one with God."[11] This unique blend of mysticism and real-life pragmatism was readily embraced by countless numbers of people. In this "spiritual rather than a religious program," they found a spiritual message that connected with their lives.

We can summarize this whole introductory section by once again focusing on what individuals are trying to affirm and what they are trying to reject when they use this phrase. Being SBNR means affirming a spiritual outlook on life: believing that our highest fulfillment comes from aligning or harmonizing ourselves with a metaphysical or unseen order to the universe. Yet being SBNR simultaneously means not feeling constrained by existing religious institutions. It is about exploring ways to bring our lives into harmony with a divine reality while doing so outside of organized religion. Being SBNR means accepting responsibility for making one's own decisions about what is real or true when it comes to our spiritual quests. As a consequence, being SBNR is intrinsically experimental, open-ended, individualistic, democratic/egalitarian, and eclectic in ways we don't typically associate with the world's major religious institutions.

In many ways, the words "religion" and "spirituality" mean the same thing. For most of history, they were nearly synonymous. They both referred to humanity's belief in the existence of a higher or unseen order and our efforts to adjust our lives such that they might align with this higher order. Historically, most people have considered themselves to be both religious and spiritual (many people still do). But over time, we have come to associate religion with what is public, shared, communal, and institutional. We have simultaneously come to associate spirituality with what is private, experiential, and free from institutional constraints. Being SBNR is about pursuing humanity's universal quest to harmonize our lives with a divine reality, but doing so in a modern world in which religious institutions have lost much of their former authority.

THE CHAPTERS AHEAD

Each chapter of this book builds another layer of sophistication onto our understanding of what it means to be SBNR. Chapter 2 (*Beginnings*) provides a brief overview of the social and cultural changes that made it difficult for many modern Americans to embrace biblical religion. It points out that the various vocabularies embraced by contemporary expressions of SBNR have long cultural histories. For example, as early as the mid-1800s, cultural luminaries such as Ralph Waldo Emerson and Henry David Thoreau popularized ways of expressing our spiritual curiosities in a bold, experimental way. The movement which they are usually associated with—the Transcendentalist movement—provided new vocabularies for describing God (e.g., Asian religions' notions of an impersonal spiritual force), our deeper spiritual nature (e.g., both Asian religions' notions of an Atman and Western esotericism's notions of aura or energy bodies), and our highest spiritual potentials (i.e., New Thought's power of positive thinking and esotericism's concept of achieving Cosmic Consciousness). Indeed, from the time of the transcendentalist movement to today, what can be called "unchurched" or nontraditional American religion is proudly eclectic. Those who are drawn to being SBNR are thus extraordinarily "combinative." By the latter term, it is meant that they are profoundly individualistic and eschew adhering to a strict or narrow set of doctrines in the ways they try to explain their spiritual nature and their relationship to the divine. Chapter 3 (*Combining Diverse Perspectives*) continues this examination by focusing on more contemporary roots (the 1960s, the rise of entheogens, the emergence of the psychological culture, the role of race and LGBT, the inclusion of feminist and ecological discourse), which similarly colluded to undermine the hegemony of organized religion while further authorizing the cultural option of being SBNR.

Chapters 1–3, then, afford us a solid historical and cultural foundation for understanding how being SBNR came to be normalized as a cultural option of expressing one's need for transcendence and meaning. They set the stage for examining the present-day spectrum of beliefs and practices associated with those who identify as being SBNR. Chapter 4 (*Being SBNR: Beliefs, Practices, Personality Profiles*) does just that by summarizing what researchers have learned about the basic belief structure of those who profess to being SBNR. It will clarify how being SBNR engages the many topics we traditionally associate with religion: God, the afterlife, sin, morality, prayer, meditation, etc. Attention will be paid to the relation between SBNR beliefs and those found in more traditional religious systems. This survey will take a look at what we know about the kinds of people who are drawn to being SBNR. Research has shown that being SBNR has a special appeal to people with specific kinds of personality traits (e.g., higher intelligence, openness to experience, the capacity for both self-forgetfulness and transpersonal identification, and a strong valuation of personal intuitions and subjective experience).

It is one thing to be able to describe what it means to be SBNR. But is it a good thing or a bad thing? Is being SBNR better or worse than the alternative viewpoints of being traditionally religious or being completely nonreligious? Chapter 5 (*Criticisms and Debates*) turns our attention to the issues that surface in these kinds of debates. SBNR has many critics. Some criticize being SBNR because it is still too religious and encourages fuzzy thoughts about supernatural realities. Yet others criticize being SBNR because it isn't religious enough and doesn't require the kinds of obedience traditionally associated with spiritual holiness. Other charges leveled against being SBNR are that it represents the increasing narcissism found in Western societies and that it valorizes the individual's own quest over commitment to the welfare of the larger community. SBNR is also prone to media-driven fads and thus lacks consistency over time. It often exhibits a superficial consumerism. And, lacking any recognized official theologians, those drawn to being SBNR are often vague about their actual beliefs and ethical principles. Additional questions abound concerning its long-term viability. At the same time, there is a counter-narrative which insists that being SBNR constitutes a stance toward life that exhibits remarkable psychological and spiritual maturity. This chapter, then, alternately presents, contests, and critiques regnant stereotypes that have emerged about being SBNR. Drawing on both past and contemporary resources, it proposes a spectrum of ways of evaluating what it means to hold the attitudes associated with being SBNR.

Chapter 6 (*Glimpsing the Future*) turns to the question of the movement's probable future(s). What features of SBNR are possibly faddish and hence unlikely to endure? Which features of SBNR are likely to become parts of our long-term cultural landscape? What might new variations of unchurched spirituality look like? Are we witnessing the birth of a new Western religious tradition and how will it relate to either traditional religious institutions or to that segment of society that has abandoned religion in favor of scientific rationality?

The final, concluding chapter (*Retracing our Steps*) will summarize the crucial features of what it means to be SBNR. In doing so, it will provide some concluding suggestions for further exploration.

NOTES

1 Several studies indicate that being SBNR should be confined, at least initially, to apply to western democracies. For example, M. Takahashi (*Religion and Spirituality in Japan.* Mystic: CT, ELM Grove Publishing, 2020) has noted that there is no equivalent noun in Japanese for the western term "spirituality," while E. Ecklund and Di Di (2018) caution that the meaning of western terms like spirituality are not readily apparent to those in Taiwan. This is not to say that a term like SBNR is not useful but rather that the meaning of a term like "spirituality" is at the very least embedded enough in often unique socio-historical and religious contexts as to make any simple claim to universality problematic. A good deal of ethnographic study is needed to ascertain how a term like SBNR translates, if at all. As a result, one cannot, at this juncture, insist that SBNR is a global phenomenon. This book, then, concentrates on western democracies, especially the United States. We concur, absent further studies, that one must be careful to avoid essentialism and colonialist adventures when using the term.

2 See, for example, Brian J. Zinnbauer et al., "Religion and Spirituality: Unfuzzying the Fuzzy," *Journal for the Scientific Study of Religion*, 36 (Dec. 1997); Courtney Bender, *The New Metaphysicals: Spirituality and the American Religious Imagination* (Chicago, IL: The University of Chicago Press, 2010); Linda Mercadante, *Belief without Borders: Inside the Minds of the Spiritual but Not Religious* (New York, NY: Oxford University Press, 2014); and Paul Heelas, ed. *Spirituality in the Modern World.* 4 vols. (New York, NY: Routledge 2012).

3 William James, *The Varieties of Religious Experience* (New York, NY: Modern Library, 1929), p. 53.

4 Louis Bouyer, "Mysticism: An Essay on the History of the Word," in R. Woods, ed., *Understanding Mysticism* (Garden City, NJ: Image Books, 1980), pp. 52–53.

5 William James, *The Varieties of Religious Experience* (New York, NY: Modern Library, 1929), p. 34.

6 *The American Mercury*, Oct. 9, 1926, p. 234.

7 See Leigh Schmidt, *Restless Souls: The Making of American Spirituality* (San Francisco, CA: Harper, 2005); W.B. Parsons ed., *Being Spiritual but Not Religious* (New York, NY: Routledge, 2018).

8 Cited in Ernest Kurtz, *Not-God: A History of Alcoholics Anonymous* (Center City, MN: Hazelden Press, 1979), pp. 19–20.

9 Bill W., cited in Ernest Kurtz, *Not-God: A History of Alcoholics Anonymous* (Center City, MN: Hazelden Press, 1979), p. 177.

10 Bill W., cited in Ernest Kurtz, *Not-God: A History of Alcoholics Anonymous* (Center City, MN: Hazelden Press, 1979), p. 179.

11 Bill W., *Twelve Steps and Twelve Traditions* (New York, NY: Alcoholics Anonymous, 1952), p. 53.

BIBLIOGRAPHY

Bender, C. *The New Metaphysicals: Spirituality and the American Religious Imagination*. Chicago, IL: The University of Chicago Press, 2010.

Bouyer, L. "Mysticism: An Essay on the History of the Word," in R. Woods, ed., *Understanding Mysticism*. Garden City, NJ: Image Books, 1980, pp. 42–56.

De Certeau, M. "Mysticism." *Diacritics*, 22, no. 2 (1992): 11–25.

Ecklund, E. and D. Di. "Global Spirituality Among Scientists," in W.B. Parsons, ed., *Being Spiritual but Not Religious*. New York, NY: Routledge, 2018, pp. 163–178.

Fuller, R. *Spiritual, But Not Religious: Understanding Unchurched America*. New York, NY: Oxford University Press, 2001.

Heelas, P. ed. *Spirituality in the Modern World*. 4 vols. New York, NY: Routledge 2012.

James, W. *The Varieties of Religious Experience*. New York, NY: Modern Library, 1929.

Kurtz, E. *Not-God: A History of Alcoholics Anonymous*. Center City, MN: Hazelden Press, 1979.

Mercadante, L. "The Seeker Next Door," *The Christian Century*, May 30 (2012), pp. 30–33.

Mercadante, L. *Belief without Borders: Inside the Minds of the Spiritual but Not Religious*. New York, NY: Oxford University Press, 2014.

Parsons, W.B. *The Enigma of the Oceanic Feeling*. New York, NY: Oxford University Press, 1999.

Parsons, W.B. ed. *Being Spiritual but Not Religious: Past, Present, Future(s)*. New York, NY: Routledge, 2018.

Schmidt, L. *Restless Souls: The Making of American Spirituality*. San Francisco, CA: Harper, 2005.

Takahashi, M. *Religion and Spirituality in Japan*. Mystic, CT: ELM Grove Publishing, 2020.

Woods, R. ed. *Understanding Mysticism*. Garden City, NJ: Routledge, 2018.

Zinnbauer, B., C. Bender L. Mercadante, P. Heelas, W. James, and E. Kurtz. "Religion and Spirituality: Unfuzzying the Fuzzy." *Journal for the Scientific Study of Religion* , 36 (Dec. 1997): 549–564.

SBNR'S BEGINNINGS

We have seen that the term "spirituality" has shifted from being under the control of institutional religion to decidedly unchurched, nontraditional, and eclectic. We might ask: what social and cultural factors helped to facilitate this shift away from church-based religion? Who have been the most eloquent champions of this shift?

THE HISTORICAL DOMINANCE OF INSTITUTIONAL RELIGION

There is a story behind the emergence of SBNR as we know it today. The story begins with a quick reminder that institutional religion has dominated the religious life of Western culture (i.e., Europe and North America) for the last two thousand years. Christianity has enjoyed a near monopoly in Western life. Judaism has rarely represented more than 3% of Western populations. Islam even less. It is thus not surprising that Christian religious groups have been among the most powerful agents of socialization in almost every Western nation. Local churches shape their members' beliefs and behavior in a variety of ways. Weekly sermons, religious education classes, group Bible reading, and hymn singing help ensure that everyone shares a common faith. Church communities are also able to exert social pressure on individuals in ways that force conformity. This is especially true in smaller towns where clergy and church members readily monitor their neighbors' behaviors. The need for social approval is a powerful

DOI: 10.4324/9781003604259-2

incentive for individuals to conform to accepted doctrinal and moral norms.

This ability to socialize individuals into a common way of life has enabled Christianity to play an important role in the histories of both Europe and North America. Western European countries emerged in eras dominated by Roman Catholicism, while Eastern European countries were influenced by varying combinations of Roman Catholicism and Orthodox Christianity. Both of these forms of Christianity had clear-cut lines of authority. At the top of the organizational power structure was the Bishop of Rome, who was commonly referred to as the Pope (in the case of Orthodox Christianity, the highest-ranking bishop was the Archbishop of Constantinople). Directly under the highest-ranking bishop were lower bishops. Under these bishops came priests who presided over each local parish church. And under the priests came the average church member. Authority was hierarchical in that it flowed from the top to the bottom of the organizational pyramid. Being religious was first and foremost about being obedient to religious authorities and their teachings.

In the early 1500s, a Catholic priest by the name of Martin Luther upset the Roman Catholic Church's monopoly on religious authority. His "protest" centered on the Church's interpretation of a few key Biblical passages, the notion of papal infallibility, the notion that "works" and the buying of "indulgences" could ensure salvation, and what was perceived to be corruption and a misleading theology. In so doing, this new theology emboldened many European Christians to form new Protestant Christian organizations. Soon, Europe witnessed the spread of new Christian institutions such as the Lutherans, Presbyterians, Baptists, the Anglican Church, and Methodists. But these new Protestant churches did not wholly undercut the fundamental premise that religion emphasized obedience to authority. Protestants instead clarified what they deemed to be the true nature of religious authority, and in doing so cast suspicion on the trustworthiness of the institutional church and its ordained clergy. Protestant leaders proclaimed that Christianity's authority lay in being justified by faith alone

(Sola Fide) in conjunction with Scripture (though in practice, this usually implied the authority of the ministers who interpreted the Bible for members of their local church).

European governments valued the way that these religious groups cultivated obedience to authority. Most of these governments aligned themselves with a specific religious institution and supported it with public funds. Hence, France was officially Roman Catholic until its revolutionary reforms in the late eighteenth century, Greece was officially Orthodox, Scotland was officially Presbyterian, Finland and Sweden both officially Lutheran, and England supported the Anglican Church (known as the Episcopal Church in some nations). Many of the "founding fathers" argued that the newly formed United States should also have a national church, though they could not agree on which of the many Protestant churches scattered throughout the colonies should be selected. The United States was thus somewhat unique among Western nations in creating a "religious marketplace," buttressed by First Amendment rights, in which religious groups needed to compete for new adherents. This created a cultural environment that fostered religious innovation and openly invited individuals to make personal choices—an environment that would make the eventual emergence of the SBNR movement more conspicuous.

ECONOMIC CONDITIONS THAT FAVOR THE EMERGENCE OF SBNR

There have, of course, always been people who are skeptical of institutional religion. Famous European intellectuals living during the Renaissance and Enlightenment (e.g., Montaigne, Diderot, and Voltaire) stand out among those willing to risk social disapproval and voice their serious doubts about the validity of the Church and its teachings. Benjamin Franklin, Thomas Jefferson, and Thomas Paine were among the well-known critics of organized religion in early American history. And, too, many everyday citizens have harbored serious doubts about some church teachings or leaders. Yet few people have ever publicly declared themselves nonbelievers or as adherents of an alternative religious philosophy.

Society as a whole is suspicious of nonbelievers. We must remember that religion consists of beliefs, not evidence-based facts. Pledging religious faith is thus an act that demonstrates willingness to submit to "groupthink." For this reason, nonbelievers are typically deemed not to be trustworthy members of the group. Nonbelievers are viewed with suspicion because they won't publicly surrender their own opinions in favor of the group's beliefs. This is an important reason why most of us are reluctant to announce any interest in diverse religious philosophies.

Some social and economic conditions make it a bit easier for individuals to think independently about religion. We are wired to avoid risks, and this is especially the case when we face stressful circumstances such as poor health or economic insecurity. But whenever people enjoy relative freedom from existential stress, we become less afraid of risk and thus more likely to consider ideas or behaviors that would set them apart from mainstream social practices. It is thus not surprising that the boldest spokespersons for alternative religious philosophies (e.g., Ralph Waldo Emerson, William James, Voltaire, Diderot) have typically come from the upper social and economic classes. Wealthier individuals are also most likely to have had formal education and access to books advocating bold and unconventional ideas.

As the Industrial Revolution increased the wealth of Western nations, a new middle class emerged that included large numbers of people who were reasonably free from the constant fear of hunger, homelessness, violence, or disease. They also gained greater access to education and opportunities to learn about unconventional ideas. Greater economic and social stability bred more confidence and optimism about the future. Middle-class citizens consequently felt less dependent on religion as their only hope. Even today, institutional religion thrives in regions that experience high levels of existential stress (i.e., poverty, crime, poorer educational opportunity). And, both in the United States and across Western Europe, interest in institutional religion declines among those with lower levels of existential stress. The point here is that as citizens of Western nations have gradually gained more social and economic well-being, they have also gradually drifted away from traditional religion.

Modern social conditions have also weakened the socialization powers of institutional religion. Church communities that could effectively monitor their members' lives in smaller, rural areas lost a lot of this ability to control people in larger, urban settings. People can live their lives more anonymously. The eventual rise of the internet provided yet another kind of space where individuals were free to explore and to express themselves without fear that they would become targets of rumors and social disapproval. As a consequence, churches have far less ability to channel their members into prescribed lifestyles. And, at the same time, individuals find themselves free to experiment with a range of spiritual beliefs and practices their ancestors would never have learned about.

EARLY AMERICAN STRANDS OF SBNR

The various religious philosophies that we associate with the SBNR movement have long histories that stretch back hundreds and perhaps even thousands of years. Scholarly volumes by Wouter Hanegraaff and Michael Horton trace the early origins of unconventional mystical systems in European history.[1] Catherine Albanese has similarly provided a detailed history of SBNR-related traditions throughout American cultural history.[2]

We might skip closer to our own era and briefly note that early European migrants to the North American colonies were not particularly interested in joining churches. Most came to the New World to seek economic opportunities unavailable to them in the more rigid social systems entrenched in Europe. In the late 1600s, less than a third of all adult colonists belonged to a church. This percentage actually declined over the next hundred years. By the time of the Revolutionary War, only about 15% of colonists were church members. It would not be until the 1840s that church attendance would rise to levels rivaling those of post-Second World War America.

This is not to suggest that colonial Americans were completely unreligious. Most engaged in prayer, and most families owned a Bible. They were enculturated into traditional Western concepts of God and the biblical accounts of the life and teachings of Jesus, even if they didn't regularly attend formal worship services. And, importantly, colonial Americans believed in the existence of supernatural powers or forces. Most believed in astrology. Horoscopes and astrological charts were printed in many of the colonial era's best-selling almanacs, making it possible for individuals to plan their commercial, agricultural, and romantic affairs with the aid of supernatural information. They were equally interested in divination practices. Fortune-tellers claimed they had special powers and were consulted for almost every kind of everyday activities, ranging from finding lost objects to discovering underground sources of water. Almost every person in this era also believed in the reality of witchcraft. Witchcraft really came down to the almost universal belief that certain individuals could harness supernatural power by using charms, conjures, and spells. Witches were thus not so much a distinct category of occult practitioners, but rather one of many varieties of "cunning persons" who drew on supernatural power to influence specific worldly activities. The infamous witchcraft trials at Andover and Salem focus attention on colonial fear of witchcraft. The truth is, however, that almost every colonist believed that astrology, divination, and sorcery were all occasionally effective methods for predicting or controlling their fates. And thus, although few Americans would ever have labeled themselves as witches, a majority nonetheless implicitly affirmed the basic belief system underlying the practice of witchcraft.

Colonial-era healing practices were also rife with supernatural elements. European immigrants brought with them a host of beliefs concerning the role that supernatural forces had in producing illness of every kind. It was common for persons to resort to conjurers or witches who prepared charms that were deemed capable of fending off malevolent supernatural influences. Consider, for example, the "powow" healing system utilized by Pennsylvania Germans. The powow system haphazardly borrowed from Christianity, popular magic, and even Native-American understandings of supernatural influence. Powow healing books encouraged readers to understand themselves as living at a precarious juncture between the natural and supernatural realms and offered strategies for fending off injurious forces that might otherwise act upon them. African Americans also took an eclectic approach to healing that utilized herbal remedies, potions, chanting, charms, amulets, and sundry occult rituals.

Interest in magic and the occult was as prevalent among the upper classes as it was among the common folk. The inventories of private library collections that have survived from the seventeenth and eighteenth centuries indicate that it was common for the most affluent members of society to own books describing occult practices. Typical of the books listed in these inventories were medical books written by the era's astrologer-physicians. Many colonists also avidly collected books dealing with astrology, alchemy, Hermeticism, Rosicrucianism, and a variety of decidedly non-Christian mystical philosophies. There is ample evidence, then, that from the very beginning, Americans have shown interest in religious ideas that had nothing to do with the doctrines officially proclaimed by the Christian faith.

There were relatively few Jews present in the colonial era, and it wasn't until the end of the nineteenth century that the Jewish population in the United States got anywhere near its current level of about 2.8%. Most American Jews during the early American period embraced the kind of open, culturally accommodating views we came to identify as Reform Judaism. The Reform tradition separates the religiosity of Jews in the ancient world from what they deem appropriate for Jews living in the modern world. Reform leaders encouraged Jews to view the Bible in its historic setting and freely reinterpret or even ignore passages that don't connect with modern understandings. In this sense, Reform Judaism actually encouraged its congregants to adopt an SBNR-like attitude toward adapting their religious beliefs to the changing conditions in which they lived. Both American and European Jews have historically been curious about spiritual beliefs and practices from across the world. Some, too, have dabbled in various esoteric philosophies such as Kabballah.

Yet another kind of religiosity existed outside the Protestant and Catholic churches of colonial North America—the religiosity of Native Americans. We need to be careful, however, about assuming that there was ever any one "Native American religion." Native Americans belonged to over one thousand distinctly separate ethnic groups. They lived in geographically separated regions and spoke hundreds of different languages. Some were hunting and gathering societies, while others developed advanced agricultural economies. It is therefore difficult—perhaps impossible—to make tidy generalizations about the religious perspectives held by these diverse native peoples. In general, however, they believed in the supernatural world, populated by various powers that were variously understood in personal terms (gods and spirits) or impersonal terms (invisible energies and influences). This supernatural world could, at any moment, break into the natural universe and produce wide-ranging beneficial or harmful effects. Religion, therefore, included making ritual use of any number of techniques that might elicit beneficial effects or ward off any potentially hazardous incursion from the spirit world. Although few texts were produced—much less survive intact—by these ancient peoples, the twentieth century witnessed a revival of interest in these ritual practices as evidenced in the popularity of Carlos Castaneda's highly romanticized accounts of a Native American shaman titled *The Teachings of Don Juan: A Yaqui Way of Knowledge.*

By the year that the United States ratified its constitution, there were almost 700,000 slaves among its population. This number would grow to about 3.2 million slaves by the 1860s. Some of these slaves were natives of both North and South America. But the majority were of African descent, with many of these having lived one or more generations in various Caribbean lands. Much as with Native Americans, their ethnic origins, languages, and customs were diverse. And, as with Native Americans, few texts survived that might help us better reconstruct the many religious perspectives held by these diverse peoples. A helpful generalization is that the African American populations also assumed that the natural world was surrounded by an invisible supernatural world that held both beneficial and harmful powers. Every effort (charms, incantations, ritual gestures, potions) must be taken to attract good fortune and ward off sinister influence. We might consider, for example, the Caribbean origins of Vodou. Vodou was understood by its creators as a fully articulated understanding of the Christianity that African slaves were taught by their New World owners. Vodou asserts that the God of the Christian Bible is the creator of both the physical universe and the world of spirits, which He made to help Him govern humanity. The goal of Vodou practices is to "serve the spirits" by offering prayers and performing ritual actions that will earn the spirits' favor and protection. Most of these spirits were equated with specific Catholic saints of whom they had learned about during their exposure to Christian teachings.

We can see, then, that by the early 1800s, Americans were already well familiar with a variety of supernatural beliefs and practices that originated far beyond the official teachings of the Christian Church. People flirted with these diverse ideas and dabbled with these diverse practices as their moods and circumstances dictated. Human culture has always been *syncretistic* in that over time, it takes beliefs originating in very different settings and gradually weaves them together in a new religious tapestry. Vodou is a prime example of how religious syncretism blends very different religious philosophies together in the span of just a few generations. In fact, Christianity itself is the syncretistic blending of various Jewish and Greek concepts that somehow came together in the teachings of Paul. Later generations gradually added Germanic paganism into the Christian mix as they came to proclaim the Winter Solstice as the season to celebrate the birth of Christ and to do so by decorating homes in greenery, exchanging gifts, and hosting festive meals. Christian Easter, with its incorporation of bunnies and eggs, wedded Christian teachings of renewal with pagan rituals of spring fertility.

Religions are, and always have been, the result of syncretism. The SBNR movement has been no exception. What might be slightly unique about the SBNR movement is the fact that most of its adherents were consciously aware that they were picking and choosing spiritual messages that appealed to them. We often use the word *eclectic* to refer to a person who self-consciously mixes and matches different styles to suit their often-changing interests. We thus refer to people as having an eclectic art collection or having an eclectic taste in music. Those drawn to the SBNR perspective are what might be called *spiritually eclectic*. They have lived in an era in which access to information (printed, delivered in live lectures, on the internet, etc.) about off-the-beaten-path spiritual philosophies gave them more opportunities to become spiritually eclectic than any previous time in history.

The concepts of religious syncretism and spiritual eclecticism might be blended into a single term that explains the very heart of what it means to be SBNR—*combinativeness*. The religious historian Catherine Albanese first suggested that human beings are almost endlessly combinative. We are motivated to meet pressing needs. We hope to stay safe, recover from illness, be economically successful, and have fulfilling romantic or personal relationships. We might, additionally, hope to secure a heavenly afterlife, ward off sinister influences, or align ourselves with God's providential powers. We try to meet these needs through any combination of tools at our disposal. We care less about theological consistency than finding what works in our lives. For this reason, we continuously combine beliefs and practices that originated from very different sources. Humans are endlessly combinative, and SBNR represents a broad spectrum of the religious ideas and practices that began circulating in popular culture during the latter half of the nineteenth century.

SBNR'S MOST INFLUENTIAL EARLY SPOKESPERSON: RALPH WALDO EMERSON

Ralph Waldo Emerson (1803–1882) was the son of the minister of Boston's First Church. Even though his father died when Ralph was young, his family had sufficient wealth to provide him with a comfortable life. He went to Harvard University, where he studied classical literature and philosophy, as was common among the nation's cultural elite. After college, he enrolled in Harvard Divinity School, where he was eventually ordained as a Unitarian minister. Just three years into his role as a minister at Boston's Second Church, he confessed that he found religion completely boring. He found formal worship services cold and lifeless. He admitted that he could no longer force himself to say he believed in a Bible written two thousand years earlier. So he resigned and left the Christian ministry forever.

But what would come next? What did he stand for? Science struck him as a far more promising route to knowledge and human betterment. Yet Western science operated on the philosophical premise that all knowledge derives from direct sense experience (meaning that we learn only through the five physical senses of sight, sound, smell, taste, and touch). Emerson could only agree with this to a point. His own personal experiences convinced him that there is more to the universe than can be detected through the physical senses alone. He was thus spiritual to his very core, even though he couldn't align his spirituality with either the established religion or the established science of his day. He was spiritually restless, yearning for a mode of personal spirituality capable of unleashing humanity's highest intellectual and emotional powers.

A few years later, in 1836, Emerson published a thin book titled *Nature*. This book ignited a fire in his contemporaries' religious imaginations. It held out an exciting vision of God's presence in the natural world. Indeed, Emerson proclaimed that when he walked alone in a forest, he opened up to an immediate sense of divine presence. The sacredness he encountered in nature contrasted sharply with the coldness of ordinary church services. He wrote that a spiritual energy surrounds us. It is everywhere and always available to us if we but let go of our rigid fixation on the world as apprehended solely through the five physical senses. If we learn to put aside our worldly rationality and open our inner spiritual faculties, we will immediately be filled with higher spiritual energies. Amerson found that, for him, simply walking quietly in nature helped him to let go of his egotistical mindset and to become inwardly receptive. As he put it, when alone in nature, "all mean egotism vanishes. I become a transparent eyeball, I am nothing; I see all; the currents of the Universal Being circulate through me; I am part and parcel of God."[3]

In one quick stroke, Emerson had cut a new spiritual path for anyone feeling limited by both the science and the biblical religion of their day. His vision of God's presence in the natural world did not ask people to denounce scientific rationality; only to expand upon it. It didn't require belief in the Bible. Nor did it portray humans as wretched sinners who needed to repent and seek a Heavenly Father's forgiveness. It asked instead that we learn to become "nothing" in the sense of letting go of our everyday mindset. By becoming nothing, we become open and receptive to the in-streaming currents of Universal Being. Emerson had staked out a new, unchurched spirituality. He offered his audiences the possibility of achieving a mystical connection with God without requiring them to dwell upon their personal sinfulness or to surrender their freedom of thought.

The same year that Emerson published *Nature*, a group comprising mostly rebellious Unitarian ministers gathered in the home of George Ripley. The group called themselves "The Transcendental Club." The club included some of the period's greatest thinkers: Ralph Waldo Emerson, Theodore Parker, James Freeman Clarke, William Henry Channing, and Orestes Brownson. They were soon joined by Henry David Thoreau, Bronson Alcott, Margaret Fuller, and Elizabeth Peabody. Soon, their ideas about religion came to be known as "Transcendentalism." These bold thinkers didn't attempt to forge a complete consensus among themselves. They valued every person's freedom to decide what was true for herself or himself. What they did hold in common was the belief that there is an order of truth which transcends the sphere of the external senses. For them, the truth of religion does not depend on ancient scriptures or formal institutions but instead upon each individual's experience of this higher spiritual order.

Emerson and his fellow Transcendentalists provided their followers with three new principles that might guide their religious explorations: (1) thinking of God as an impersonal spiritual energy rather than a heavenly male ruler; (2) envisioning a multi-level universe that contains many realms or dimensions extending beyond the grasp of our physical senses; and (3) anticipating the possibility that under the right conditions, we can achieve an inward harmony with these "higher" realms and experience an inflow or influx of spiritual energies into our mental and physical lives.

Emerson's greatest contribution to the emerging SBNR movement was the way he encouraged people to think about God in fresh, new ways. The God of the Bible is a symbol of masculine power: a Father who has power over a family, a ruler who has power over a kingdom, a Supreme Being who dominates all lower beings, or a Judge who has power to sentence and punish individuals for legal transgressions. Emerson encouraged his readers to envision God as a power that energizes us from within. In the passage we cited above, Emerson portrayed God in terms of "the currents of the Universal Being" that circulate through us when we become inwardly receptive. Emerson had read Hindu scriptures called the Upanishads that describe God as the infinite, impersonal spirit known as Brahman. Emerson translated the concept of Brahman into English as the Over-Soul. The metaphor of Over-Soul provides a succinct image of how each of us is connected with the all-embracing spirit of God. In the Transcendentalist view, knowing God doesn't have anything to do with memorizing Bible passages or church creeds. Instead, knowing God means discovering that we are always and everywhere in continuous harmony with God if we can but quiet our outer mind. Depicting God as the Over-Soul suggests that we have the capacity to receive what Emerson described as "an influx of the Divine mind into our mind."

This new way of viewing God rendered Biblical religion obsolete. The Bible demands that humans both worship and obey a powerful Father who art in Heaven. The Bible further tells humans that they are sinners, and will thus go to Hell upon death unless they lower themselves before God and ask for forgiveness. But whereas the Bible tells us that we are separated from God by sin, the Transcendentalists stated that we are only separated from God by limited self-awareness. If we learn to open up those levels of the mind that go deeper than the physical senses, we will simultaneously find ourselves inwardly connected to the divine. Emerson wrote in glowing terms how finding ourselves receptive to the inflow of Universal Being is an ecstatic religious event. It is marked by "that shudder of awe and delight with which the individual soul always mingles with the Universal Soul."[4]

The Transcendentalists' second principle, the conviction that the universe contains higher spiritual dimensions that transcend the physical senses, distinguished it from being a purely secular or nonreligious philosophy. It was, to its core, a metaphysical vision of the self and the wider universe. Emerson's notion of the multidimensional nature of the universe was derived in part from the Swedish mystic Emanuel Swedenborg. Swedenborg (1688–1772) was a preeminent European scientist when he claimed to have been visited by angelic beings. Swedenborg's angelic guides taught him that the universe consists of seven interpenetrating dimensions that were in some fundamental way in correspondence with one another. This doctrine of metaphysical correspondence explained that whenever these dimensions come into harmonious connection with one another, energies from "higher" dimensions can flow into—and causally influence—"lower" dimensions. This principle of metaphysical correspondence or harmony has proven very suggestive to the SBNR imagination over the years. To some, it has been implied that there are other spiritual dimensions containing angels or other ascended beings from whom we might receive otherwise secretive spiritual teachings. To others, it has been suggested that the physical human body is but one of the soul's many bodies (i.e., etheric or astral bodies) from which we might receive life-enhancing vitality or guidance. And to yet others, it has suggested that we are connected to the spirit world in which the souls of beloved friends and relatives reside.

The Transcendentalists' third principle was that of discovering techniques for establishing harmonious connection with higher metaphysical dimensions in order to induce the influx of spiritual energies into our mental and physical lives. This principle has proven equally capable of generating new and innovative spiritual practices over the course of SBNR history. Being SBNR is, above all else, about discovering techniques that foster inward receptivity and thereby opening ourselves up to higher metaphysical energies. For

Emerson, this might mean walking alone through the woods in an effort to let go of our preoccupation with our material selves. For others, it has meant learning techniques (e.g., meditation) to enter into mystical states of consciousness. Even some forms of "body practice," such as massage therapies, are founded on the principle that they align our many metaphysical bodies in ways that restore the flow of health-giving energies. The founder of Chiropractic Medicine, D.D. Palmer, created his therapeutic system on the belief that our bodies are designed to receive inflows of divine spirit that then travels through and energizes our entire physiology. He reasoned that any blockage to our spinal column disrupts this natural metaphysical harmony and thereby results in disease. The whole system of chiropractic manipulations of the spine was designed as a technique for restoring the harmonious reception and flow of metaphysical energies throughout the physical body. Alternative medical practices that utilize crystal stones, special colors, or special aromas are likewise among the many SBNR variations of this enduring principle of metaphysical correspondence.

THE SPREAD OF METAPHYSICAL CURIOSITY

Emerson and his fellow Transcendentalists were among America's social and intellectual elite. They were well-educated and relatively affluent. For this reason, their spiritual outlook had an upper-class feel to it and attracted those who possessed the time and resources to explore the subtleties of spiritual philosophy. But, as it turns out, the Transcendentalists' three main principles (images of god as an impersonal energy; the existence of multiple spiritual dimensions; and the possibility of becoming receptive to the inflow of spiritual energy) quickly filtered into several newly emerging movements that reached more deeply into the vocabularies with which middle-class people might think about themselves and their relationship to God. Mesmerism, Spiritualism, and Theosophy attracted fairly large followings in the latter part of the 1800s, and each helped popularize a cluster of metaphysical concepts that shape SBNR spirituality to this day.

Franz Anton Mesmer (1734–1815) was a medical doctor in Vienna, Austria, who claimed that he discovered the presence of an ultrafine fluid he called *animal magnetism*. He picked this term because he was convinced that this invisible fluid was present in every living creature and that it responded to magnetic influence. Mesmer further postulated that animal magnetism exists in an etheric dimension undetectable by the five physical senses. He believed that this energetic power flows from this etheric dimension into our physical bodies, imparting both health and vitality. He also reasoned that human bodies would become sick if, for any reason, we were to become disconnected from this vital force or if its flow throughout our bodies were to become blocked. What came to be known as mesmerism was the set of techniques Mesmer developed to supercharge a person's nervous system with this mysterious life-enhancing energy.

Originally, Mesmer passed magnets up and down his patients' spinal columns in an effort to induce an inflow of animal magnetism. Over time, however, he and his followers shifted their attention to putting patients into a sleep-like trance. It was thought that this trance enabled patients to become more receptive to the inflow of vital magnetic energy. While in this trance-like state, they were aware of nothing except the voice and commands of the healer (mesmerist). Yet, when they returned to their normal waking state, they felt refreshed and claimed either partial or complete recovery from their physical ailments. More astonishing was the claim that about 10% of all mesmerized persons spontaneously demonstrated extraordinary mental powers. Stories abounded of mesmerized subjects who suddenly became capable of extrasensory perception, such as telepathy or clairvoyance. Some even claimed that being mesmerized enabled them to become filled with the Holy Spirit, bringing about an immediate moral and spiritual transformation. In the twinkling of an eye, people could undergo a total renewal—physical, mental, and spiritual. And this was accomplished without asking people to repent, to accept any formal doctrine, or to join any religious organization.

Stage demonstrations of mesmerism were great entertainment. Deft showmanship enabled traveling mesmerists to dazzle audiences with their ability to unleash the hidden powers of the human mind. All the while, they introduced wider segments of society to the concept that, under the right circumstances, humans can become inwardly receptive to the inflow of higher energies. One audience member was a clockmaker from Belfast, Maine by the name of Phineas P. Quimby. Quimby was emboldened to take up the practice of mesmerism himself and was soon giving his own lecture-demonstrations on the science of animal magnetism. Quimby, however, came to a novel interpretation of why humans fell ill in the first place. He reasoned that our waking minds (i.e., our beliefs and attitudes) control the degree to which we remain in harmony—or fall out of harmony—with this instreaming vital force. A positive, optimistic attitude lawfully results in spiritually driven vitality. Negative or materialistic attitudes lawfully render us depleted of life-giving energies. In this sense, he became the "Scientist of Transcendentalism" in that he boiled abstract metaphysics down to a simple technique: the power of positive thinking.

Quimby's theories about the role of right thinking weren't scientific in the normal sense of the word. But they worked. What Quimby called his science of Mind Cure seemingly demonstrated the principle of cause and effect. Moreover, Quimby contrasted Mind Cure with biblical religion which he deemed the source of most people's fearful stance toward life. Quimby once estimated that a full half of all disease stemmed from the fears and timidity that his patients acquired from church-based religion. To dissolve his patient's fears, Quimby had to teach them that spiritual power was immediately available to them if they but looked within. He followed the Transcendentalists in viewing Christ as the great example—not the great exception—of human nature. By this, Quimby meant that Jesus was a man of flesh and blood like anyone else, except that he learned to channel "the God in us all." Mind Cure philosophy could thus be understood as a progressive application of what Christianity had been trying to communicate all along.

Quimby died in 1866. His disorganized set of written notes remained unpublished. Yet he had healed hundreds, perhaps thousands of patients who returned home talking about his system of ideas. A few of Quimby's patients stayed in close contact with him and took it upon themselves to become ambassadors of the Mind Cure philosophy. It was through these former patients that Quimby's teachings gained wider audiences. The best-known of them was Mary Baker Eddy, who transformed Quimby's teachings into the Church of Christ, Scientist (commonly known as Christian Science). In 1875, Eddy published her most important work, *Science and Health with Key to the Scriptures*, which sold over 400,000 copies by the end of the nineteenth century. Yet three of Quimby's other patient-disciples proved even more successful in spreading metaphysical spirituality to middle-class citizens. Anetta Dresser, her husband Julius, and colleague Warren Felt Evans wrote dozens of books and delivered hundreds of public lectures that stretched Quimby's Mind Cure philosophy into what became known as the New Thought movement. New converts to the New Thought message believed that they had discovered a religious message that enlivened their everyday lives. What is more, they believed that its message of finding mental harmony with an immanent divine power was thoroughly lawful, as precise as the laws of physics or chemistry. One of New Thought's most successful authors, Ralph Waldo Trine, put this harmonial science succinctly in his bestselling book *In Tune with the Infinite*:

> The great central fact in human life is the coming into a conscious vital realization of our oneness with the Infinite Life, and the opening of ourselves fully to the Divine inflow. In just the degree that we come into a conscious realization of our oneness with the Infinite Life, and open ourselves to the Divine inflow, do we … exchange dis-ease for ease, inharmony for harmony, suffering and pain for health and strength. To recognize our own divinity and our intimate relation to the Universal, is to attach the belt of our machinery to the power-house of the Universe.[5]

What the New Thoughters and the Transcendentalists studiously avoided, however, was making any reference to the existence of angels, spirits, or any other kind of personal entities who might be residing in higher metaphysical realms. Most of them considered such a belief to be crass superstition and thus wholly incompatible with what they proclaimed as a co-scientific spiritual outlook. But, as it turned out, an itinerant mesmerist passed through Poughkeepsie, New York in 1843. Seventeen-year-old Andrew Jackson Davis attended this lecture-demonstration on the science of animal magnetism and decided to begin experimenting with mesmeric trances on his own. Davis reports that he successfully entered the deepest levels of trance and was able to perform such mental feats as reading from books while blindfolded, telepathically receiving thoughts from other people, or traveling clairvoyantly to distant locales. He proved so adept at entering the mesmeric trance that he hired himself out as a professional subject, exhibiting his miraculous powers.

After several months of repeated journeys into the deepest recesses of his mind, Davis began making contact with the souls of deceased philosophers and theologians. Davis proclaimed that the mesmeric trance state can open up direct communication with the spirit world—a world populated with the souls of deceased human beings. A new metaphysical system—spiritualism—was born. Intellectually oriented people found that spiritualism synthesized mesmerism, Swedenborgianism, and Transcendentalism into a cohesive metaphysical philosophy. But most people responded to spiritualism's belief in the existence of spirit guides who take a personal interest in our lives. Spiritualism provided assurance in everlasting life. Moreover, it also provided opportunities to make contact with our loved ones and receive both comfort and advice.

A few features of spiritualist philosophy stand out. First, spiritualism embraced science as a reliable path to discovering the lawful principles regulating the universe (of course, implying that science would have to expand its scope to include recognition of metaphysical spheres of existence). Second, spiritualism emphasized the principle of spiritual progress. The whole purpose of creation is to provide us opportunities for growth and progress. Davis contrasted his metaphysical vision with traditional Christianity's views of heaven and hell.

Whereas Christian doctrine uses the fear of hell as its primary motivational tool, spiritualism has "perfect faith in the divinity of every man" and envisions the universe as the great training ground where we gradually learn to manifest our innate potentials. And, finally, spiritualism populates the universe with spirit beings who yearn to provide us with comfort, guidance, and wisdom. From Davis's time right up to the present day, the SBNR movement has included many transient enthusiasms for seeking the counsel of guardian angels, ascended Master Teachers, and saintly philosophers.

Alongside mesmerism's and spiritualism's role in generating metaphysical curiosity among wider ranges of Western society were the mystically charged teachings of Theosophy. Madame Helena Blavatsky (1831–1891) immigrated to New York from her native Russia in 1872. She had already traveled throughout Europe, gravitating to people who dabbled in occult philosophies. In New York, she earned a reputation as a spiritualist trance medium, channeling messages from advanced spiritual teachers whom she referred to as the mahatmas (the Hindu term for "great souls"). Madame Blavatsky soon met up with Colonel Henry S. Olcott, a lawyer who was deeply interested in the scientific and religious implications of spiritualism. Together they launched the Theosophical Society, a metaphysical organization dedicated to bridging the current gulf between science and religion through the study of mesmerism, spiritualism, and the universal ether thought to connect the corresponding spheres of the universe.

Blavatsky produced one of the most important books in the history of "combinative" spirituality, *Isis Unveiled*. Blavatsky claimed that her book consisted of messages that were dictated to her by the mahatmas, members of the Universal Mystic Brotherhood who lived in the Himalayan mountains of Tibet. The mahatmas were said to be spiritually evolved humans who had achieved the ability to travel and communicate psychically—allowing them to communicate regularly with Blavatsky whenever she entered a mystical trance. The messages they sent her explained that both Hinduism and Buddhism contained mystical truths that had hitherto eluded

Western religions. Among the Hindu concepts that they championed were belief in reincarnation and karma. They also taught Blavatsky an intricate vocabulary for referring to the many "subtle" layers of selfhood. Humans, the mahatmas taught, actually inhabit seven levels or planes of existence. Theosophy thus teaches that our physical body is connected with these metaphysical bodies through the seven *chakras* (spiritual centers) located at various points along our spinal columns. Theosophy further teaches that meditation can open up our *chakras* and thereby bring us into harmonious connection with these other metaphysical bodies. In this way, Theosophy linked mystical concepts from Asian religions with Emerson's doctrines of metaphysical correspondence and influx. By opening our *chakras*, we cultivate the inflow of subtle energies flowing from higher metaphysical levels of existence. This, as Theosophy proclaims, is the secret to physical health, emotional serenity, and perhaps parapsychological abilities.

Even at the height of its popularity, Theosophy probably never had more than 20,000 members. Yet despite these relatively small numbers, Theosophy has probably exerted more influence on the SBNR tradition than any other single metaphysical movement (except Transcendentalism). *Isis Unveiled* has alone sold over 500,000 copies to date. And Theosophy's ideas, once put into general circulation, quickly spilled over into the vocabularies used by proponents of almost every kind of SBNR spirituality. Theosophy eloquently advocated a concept that scholars call perennialism. Perennialism teaches that all world religions are the same in essence since they all begin in a single individual's mystical experience of the divine. This experience, however, is ineffable. It can never be translated into language since language depicts attributes of physical—not metaphysical—reality. It follows that even though all religions are essentially the same at their core, their various creeds will differ owing to the specifics of the cultural setting in which they first emerged.

Theosophy's claim that mystical experience is the ultimate truth of religion helped spiritual seekers believe that they were not abandoning Christianity but instead recovering its pristine core. Just as important to spiritual seekers was Theosophy's romanticization of the "mystic East." Theosophy didn't simply teach tolerance of Asian religions. It claimed that the mystical traditions within Hinduism and Buddhism were spiritually superior to Western religion. Theosophy was largely responsible for the fact that today's seekers readily adopt yoga meditation practices, speak of Zen *satori*, refer to karma or reincarnation, or believe in the existence of "subtle energies" such as *kundalini*, *qi*, or *prana*. A high percentage of the alternative healing systems (e.g., Reiki, Therapeutic Touch, chiropractic) and the human potential psychologies that comprise the contemporary SBNR spectrum have roots that can be traced directly back to Theosophy.

POINTING FORWARD

The spiritual philosophies popularized by the Transcendentalists, Theosophists, spiritualists, and other metaphysical systems injected wholly new concepts into the vocabularies with which middle-class citizens might speculate about their place in the grander universe. They made it abundantly clear that existing churches didn't hold a monopoly on spiritual truth. Most of those who were exposed to these fascinating topics were only hoping to supplement, not wholly abandon, their inherited religious affiliations. They often wondered whether their Christian (or Jewish heritage for a small segment of the population) might itself contain spiritual depths often obscured or overlooked by current church leaders. The important thing was that they were open to new insights.

NOTES

1 See Michael Horton, *Shaman and Sage: The Roots of "Spiritual but Not Religious" in Antiquity* (Grand Rapids, MI: Eerdmans, 2024) and Wouter Hanegraaff, *New Age Religion and Western Culture* (Albany, NY: State University of New York Press, 1998).
2 Catherine Albanese, *A Republic of Mind and Spirit: A Cultural History of American Metaphysical Religion* (New Haven, CT: Yale University Press, 2007).
3 Ralph Waldo Emerson, *The Complete Works of Ralph Waldo Emerson*, 12 vols. (New York, NY: AMS Press, 1968), 1:10.

4 Ralph Waldo Emerson, *The Complete Works of Ralph Waldo Emerson*, 12 vols. (New York, NY: AMS Press, 1968), 2:82.
5 Ralph Waldo Trine, *In Tune with the Infinite* (New York, NY: Crowell, 1897), p. 16.

BIBLIOGRAPHY

Albanese, C. *Nature Religion in America*. Chicago, IL: The University of Chicago Press, 1990.
Albanese, C. *A Republic of Mind and Spirit: A Cultural History of American Metaphysical Religion*. New Haven, CT: Yale University Press, 2007.
Bridges, H. *American Mysticism*. New York, NY: Harper & Row, 1970.
Emerson, R.W. *The Complete Works of Ralph Waldo Emerson*, 12 vols. New York, NY: AMS Press, 1968.
Hanegraaff, W. *New Age Religion and Western Culture*. Albany, NY: State University of New York Press, 1998.
Horton, M. *Shaman and Sage: The Roots of "Spiritual but Not Religious" in Antiquity*. Grand Rapids, MI: Eerdmans, 2024.
James, W. *The Varieties of Religious Experience*. Cambridge, MA: Harvard University Press, 1985.
Trine, R.W. *In Tune with the Infinite*. New York, NY: Crowell, 1897.

3

COMBINING DIVERSE PERSPECTIVES

Being spiritual but not religious (SBNR) has roots that go back to antiquity. Greek mystery cults and Plato's doctrines concerning the human mind's connection with higher spheres are but a few examples of what might be labeled Western culture's gnostic tradition. Working-class citizens had neither the leisure nor the opportunities for pursuing these interests in any sustained way. And, to be sure, church authorities worked hard to push these blasphemous concepts to the far periphery of respectable society. But in the nineteenth century—and especially in the United States—a widening segment of society was introduced to inspiring spiritual philosophies.

The many variations of being SBNR that we know today began to take their current forms in the later decades of the twentieth century. New social forces called traditional institutions into question. Young and old alike sought new ways of making sense of the world themselves and the world they lived in. New concerns about the environment, about gender roles, about sexual norms, and about the deepest layers of the human mind raised questions that seemingly couldn't be addressed by established religion. Spiritual restlessness gave rise to new avenues for expressing human spirituality outside the strictures of religious institutions.

COUNTERCULTURAL STREAMS: 1950–1970

After the Second World War, many Western nations sought a return to normalcy by emphasizing the importance of church membership. The United States, for example, witnessed its

DOI: 10.4324/9781003604259-3

historically highest rates of weekly church attendance in the 1950s. Being publicly affiliated with a Protestant Christian, Catholic Christian, or Jewish congregation was deemed a significant indicator of social respectability. Yet the church's validity as a source of cultural wisdom came under sustained assault as this generation's children (the so-called Baby Boomers) themselves entered adolescence and then adulthood.

Traumatic national events during the 1960s brought all cultural institutions under critical scrutiny—organized religion included. The younger generation perceived organized religion to be intertwined with the "establishment" responsible for the unpopular war in Vietnam and the harsh reality of racial segregation. Youth responded by creating what was termed the "hippie" movement that sanctioned nontraditional forms of sexuality, experiments with communal living, and the introduction of alternate political narratives. These new modes of social interaction helped propagate countercultural attitudes aimed at deconstructing traditional (and often misogynistic and prejudicial) religious narratives.

The counterculture spread through new, often revolutionary social spaces such as coffee houses, communes, rock concerts, and protest marches. Even the more entrenched social spaces and institutions, notably universities and theological seminaries, joined the attack on outmoded cultural forms. Feminists issued challenges to a religious bureaucracy created "by men and for men," existentialist philosophers articulated a "death of God" theology, and social critics of many varieties (Freud, Marx, Nietzsche) highlighted the inherently oppressive nature of religious institutions.

Added to the mix was the growing acceptance and popularity of Eastern religions. Before 1840, the western engagement with Eastern religions was sporadic and superficial. In the later part of the nineteenth century, however, a more profound series of exchanges took place, which slowly altered the socio-political and intellectual appreciation of Eastern religions. Part of this was driven by a new social base of immigrants who carried with them Eastern forms of worship. By the end of the nineteenth century, approximately one million Asians had emigrated to the United States and multiple places of worship (Buddhist, Hindu, Sikh, Confucian, and Taoist) were established. At the World's Parliament in Chicago in 1893, adepts like Vivekananda (who travelled to Harvard to meet with James) had found ways to institutionalize meditation in America. Others, such as Soyen Saku, Yogananda, and Anagarika Dharmapala, helped to secure the proliferation of Vedanta, Zen, and Yoga. This cultural soil helped to facilitate the establishment of university positions in oriental studies and comparative religion. A new generation of scholars (e.g., Hermann Oldenberg, Max Müller, Paul Deussen, Sylvian Levi, etc.) translated and disseminated the details of Eastern texts and traditions. Western intellectual figures, such as Henry Steel Olcott, Romain Rolland, Schopenhauer, and Nietzsche as well as a bevy of emerging psychologists (Carl Jung, William James, R.M. Bucke), helped to further disseminate eastern ideas into the culture at large.

Even so, the Asian Exclusion Act of 1924 (which curtailed immigration) alongside the Second World War stymied much of the advances of earlier decades. It was not until that Act was rescinded (in 1965) alongside a new wave of immigration that there was a notable resurgence in the influence of Eastern religions. This new era of revitalization was enhanced by the growing cultural fascination with a new cadre of eastern teachers and gurus. The 1960s saw the advent of Buddhist and Hindu missionaries like D.T. Suzuki, the Dalai Lama, Maharishi Mahesh Yogi, and Shunryu Suzuki Roshi, who gathered around them notable western followers (e.g., Allen Ginsburg, Timothy Leary, Aldous Huxley, Jack Kerouac, Mike Murphy, Allen Watts, the Beatles). Eastern practices, which found homes in the establishment of retreat centers like Esalen and the San Francisco Zen Center, were blessed by celebrities and intellectuals alike. Huston Smith, arguably the most influential scholar of religion during the decade of the sixties, spoke to this new cultural soil by linking the study of comparative religion and mysticism to the American counterculture's advocacy of a more individualistic, experience-driven religiosity.

Spiritual seekers turned to Eastern mystical practices in their quests for self-discovery. The fact that Eastern religions came with no fixed dogmas made it easy for them to be embraced by those who were disillusioned with the Judeo-Christian tradition. Popular spokespersons for Eastern spirituality were eager to point out connections with many emerging theories in academic psychology (e.g., William James, Karen Horney, Erich Fromm, Carl Jung). What Eastern spirituality and these new psychological theories had in common was that they proclaimed the wisdom residing deep within every human mind. Western psychologists, in turn, praised Eastern mystical and meditation practices for helping us to gain access to these powers hidden deep within ourselves. Academic institutions such as Harvard Medical School endorsed the therapeutic benefits of daily meditation practices. Researchers conducted over one thousand studies on the psychological value of Maharishi Mahesh Yogi's transcendental meditation system. This informal alliance between Eastern spiritual philosophies and Western psychologies of the inner self continued throughout the twentieth century, introducing middle-class citizens to numerous forms of meditation matching the needs of those proclaiming to be SBNR.

The counter-culture thrived in new social spaces: psychotherapy sessions, university classes, television programs, and coffee shops. Visiting a psychotherapist became a common activity among upper- and middle-class citizens during the 1950s and 1960s. One of the goals of psychotherapy is gaining new insights into our past. Patients are taught to identify the origins of their current fears, anxiety, and sense of guilt. It should come as no surprise that people often link religion to their earliest experiences of inferiority. This is especially true when women reflect on the conceptions of gender imposed on them. And this is truer still for those whose sexual leanings came under the harsh condemnation of church authorities. Counseling sessions provided a social space in which people could confront the sources of their anxiety and low self-esteem. And, with time, they learned new skills for navigating their lives independently of the beliefs or practices of organized religion.

For most of Western history, the Church paid artists to produce public works that would connect personal spiritual journeys with the institutional church. Even by the fifteenth century, however, public art emerged to appeal to the hopes and ambitions of a rising middle class. And, by the 1950s and 1960s, television and cinema offered yet additional social spaces. Among their most popular storylines were those that celebrate individuals' heroic efforts to achieve personal fulfillment even when doing so requires them to abandon traditional social conventions.

College classrooms, too, provide social spaces that foster movement away from "blind faith." Unlike churches, synagogues, or mosques, college classrooms do not proclaim religious creeds. On the contrary, they are secular, pluralistic, and, above all, critical. When one agrees to participate in the public space created by a college classroom, one has simultaneously agreed to value critical scrutiny of traditional "truths."

THE RISE OF PSYCHO-SPIRITUALITY

Prior to the advent of modern psychology, citizens of Western nations turned to religion when they were confused, lonely, or in need of an emotional pick-me-up. Ministers, priests, and rabbis offered pastoral counseling in addition to their role in worship services. The Bible was thought to be a reliable guide to understanding ourselves and the problems we face in life. Clergy counseled people with numerous worries to read Matthew 6: 19–34; people needing courage to read Joshua 1; or those pondering investments and returns to read Mark 10: 17–31. But in the twenty-first century, our cultural situation is very different. Psychology has replaced religion as the principal source of counseling and guidance. Almost all educated people have some familiarity with academic psychology. And, too, books marketed to the general reading public have provided a new stock of ideas for solving the emotional problems that arise in everyday life. Television talk shows, radio call-in programs, and innumerable self-help books provide a steady source of psychological strategies to aid us in our quests for happiness.

Psychology is a scientific field. Most psychological research and writing are on topics that have nothing to do with humanity's hunger to experience a higher, unseen order of life. But by the 1950s and 1960s, a number of psychologists turned their attention to topics that connect with human spirituality. A perfect example is Abraham Maslow. Maslow is widely considered the founder of a new branch of psychology, which he referred to as humanistic psychology. Maslow explained that while previous psychologists had focused either on psychologically ill patients or on laboratory animals, his new branch of psychology was dedicated to studying "creativity, love, self, growth, organism, basic need-gratification, self-actualization, higher values, ego-transcendence." His associate, Rollo May, described humanistic psychology as an effort to "unite science and ontology."

Maslow had already earned academic recognition through his studies on motivation. These studies led to his well-known formulation of the hierarchy of human needs. His basic hypothesis was that humans are motivated to meet their most pressing needs. The most potent needs are securing food and shelter. If these basic needs are met, we will then be motivated to meet needs that are largely social in nature, such as peer approval and self-esteem. Assuming these social needs are also satisfied, we are then motivated to pursue the "highest" needs that Maslow termed those of self-actualization. Self-actualization occurs when individuals rise above the biological and social forces that ordinarily shape their behavior. No longer a pawn under the control of instincts or social conditioning, self-actualizing individuals are free to express themselves in truly creative ways. Maslow's study of self-actualizing people led him to conclude that "humanity has a higher and transcendent nature, and that is part of their essence."[1]

Maslow found that self-actualizing people report having had intense emotional episodes that he called "peak experiences." Peak experiences are those rare moments when we cease striving and instead let go to the fullness of the moment. It is common for people having a peak experience to feel that they are momentarily connected with a reality beyond the natural universe. As Maslow put it, peak experiences take us beyond our accustomed way of viewing life and impart a vivid perception "of the whole cosmos or at least the unity and integration of it and of everything in it, including his Self."[2]

Maslow believed that his observations of peak experiences provided scientific confirmation of the perennial philosophy. That is, Maslow argued that all of the world's religions began in their founders' inward, private experiences of the sacred. He further claimed that since these experiences fall neatly within his research on peak experiences, psychological science is now able to shed light on the very origins and nature of organized religion. He explained that peak experiences are themselves the originating core of all genuine spirituality. They provide people with an intense awareness of "practically everything that Rudolf Otto defines as characteristic of the religious experience—the holy; the sacred, creature feeling, humility; gratitude and oblation; thanksgiving; awe before the *mysterium tremendum;* the sense of the divine, the ineffable."[3] Maslow further explained that organized religions begin when those who have had such peak experiences attempt to communicate their ecstatic experience to those who haven't had such experiences. Unfortunately, doctrines and creeds can never really communicate the experiential core of spiritual insight. There is thus a great divide between people who have had peak experiences (spiritual people) and those who haven't (religious people). Maslow warned his readers that organized religion is little more than

> a set of habits, behaviors, dogmas, forms, which at the extreme becomes entirely legalistic and bureaucratic, conventional, empty, and in the truest meaning of the word, anti-religious.... Organized Religion, the churches, finally may become the major enemies of the religious experience and the religious experiencer.[4]

Maslow frequently pointed to the similarities between his views and those of such writers as William James, Ralph Waldo Emerson, Walt Whitman, and the Zen philosopher D.T. Suzuki. Maslow believed that his studies of peak experiences reinforced these writers' view that spirituality has to do with adding a new zest to this life, not procuring an afterlife. Peak experiences provide the life-altering insight that "religion's Heaven is actually available in principle all through life. It is available to us now, and is all around us."[5] Humanistic psychology offered a new and psychologically phrased spiritual outlook. It encouraged people to bypass religious institutions and instead cultivate their own inner experiences of the divine.

Another of the many psychologists who came to be associated with this effort to unite science and ontology was Carl Jung. Jung was Freud's closest colleague for many years. In mid-career, however, Jung parted ways with Freud. Jung's break with Freud stemmed from their differing views of the nature of the unconscious mind. Freud's view was narrower in that it mostly associated the unconscious mind with our inherited instincts and often-hidden memories of our childhood. Jung, however, had undergone a series of paranormal experiences of his own and proclaimed that the unconscious mind extends far deeper than Freud had acknowledged.

Jung had asked himself whether he, the son of a Protestant minister, still believed in the Christian myth. As a scientifically educated physician, he knew that he didn't. He therefore attempted to develop a new spiritual vocabulary more suited to the modern world. Jung used the term "collective unconscious" to refer to the deepest level of the human mind. In his autobiography, he confessed that all along he associated the collective unconscious with the "God within." His psychological theory, therefore, focused on the role that the collective unconscious performs in linking us with deeper spiritual powers. As Jung put it, his psychological theory focused on the point where the natural and spiritual worlds connect—the deepest levels of our unconscious minds. Jung's methods for deciphering the spiritual depths of the mind found their way into Joseph Campbell's enormously popular surveys of mythology and Thomas Moore's bestselling work on finding spirituality in everyday life, *The Care of the Soul.* They were, in fact, the basis of the *Star Wars* movie references to Jedi warriors' ability to connect with "the Force."

A great many other writers also contributed to this fusion of psychology and spirituality: Viktor Frankl, Alan Watts, Ken Wilber, Stanislav Grof, Ira Progoff, Roberto Assagioli, Rollo May, and Carl Rogers. The Canadian psychologist R.M. Bucke spoke for this "tradition" when he went so far as to say that religious institutions would simply disappear as increasing numbers of Westerners experienced the mystical state he called "cosmic consciousness." Bucke contrasted traditional forms of religion with the personal enlightenment achieved in cosmic consciousness:

> It will not depend on tradition. It will not be believed or disbelieved. It will not be a part of life, belonging to certain hours, times, occasions. It will not be in sacred books nor in the mouths of priests. It will not dwell in churches and meetings and forms and days.... Churches, priests, forms, creeds, prayers, all agents, all intermediaries between the individual man and God will be permanently replaced by direct unmistakable intercourse. Sin will no longer exist nor will salvation be desired ... each soul will feel and know itself to be immortal, will feel and know that the entire universe with all its good and with all its beauty is for it and belongs to it forever.[6]

The trend toward identifying spirituality with individual mystical experiences was further disseminated through the arts, film, social media, and even psychotherapy sessions. Terms like "self-realization," "authenticity," and "peak-experiences," all of which find their origin in psycho-spirituality, became the preferred terminology for talking about one's spiritual growth.

In a sociological sense, this move towards a psychospiritual way of thinking about the self-mirrors the trend away from traditional institutions. Max Weber called attention to this when he distinguished four major social types he referred to as inner-worldly asceticism, inner-worldly mysticism, other-worldly mysticism and other-worldly asceticism. All of these types describe how individuals follow a plan or path to achieve wholeness and salvation. For example, inner-worldly mysticism is linked to the early Protestants, who felt that success in business by working long hours while not becoming attached to financial gain was a "sign" that they were predestined to heaven. Other-worldly asceticism, on the other hand, achieves the same aim but by withdrawing from the world altogether, as with the Amish. Other-worldly mysticism, best represented by the monastics, also removes one from the world, there to be convinced of salvation through mystical union with God. Finally, inner-worldly mysticism, a fairly recent phenomenon, is a modern form of adaptation to a culture characterized by the rise of capitalism, individualism, pluralism, and various introspective techniques, many of which influenced the baby-boomer generation. Inner-worldly mysticism expresses the need to work "in the world" while striving for wholeness and the actualization of the "self." Therapy, yoga, meditation, dietary and exercise programs, and the individualistic, eclectic supermarket approach to religion are part and parcel of inner-worldly mysticism.

THE LEGACY OF WILLIAM JAMES: FASCINATION WITH ALTERED STATES OF CONSCIOUSNESS

Another psychologist, William James (1842–1910), made the most enduring contributions to the SBNR tradition. William grew up in a very wealthy family. His father, Henry James Sr., had the time and resources to investigate the era's most interesting philosophies. Henry invited intellectuals of every stripe into his home to discuss controversial subjects, especially controversial religious subjects. Among Henry's frequent guests was Ralph Waldo Emerson, who may have been responsible for the James household becoming so enamored of both Swedenborgian and Transcendentalist teachings. William thus grew up in a household that encouraged speculation about the existence of higher metaphysical levels of reality and about the possibility of an "influx" of spiritual energy into our physical world.

Henry James Sr. urged his eldest son (his other son, Henry James Jr., developed into one of America's most gifted novelists) to devote himself to the era's most prestigious intellectual endeavor—science. William heeded the advice and graduated first from Harvard University's pre-med program and then Harvard's medical school. Throughout this period of his life, William was prone to poor mental and physical health. Chronic insomnia, eye trouble, digestive problems, and back pains were cruel reminders that his life just wasn't coming together the way he had hoped. He was frequently haunted by an all-encompassing sense of despair, futility, and worthlessness.

James suffered from a very modern disease: spiritual restlessness. He yearned for a grand spiritual dimension to his life, yet felt alienated from conventional religion. James felt the absence of God. Sadly, though, his father's metaphysical philosophies seemed too speculative to offer him any reliable hold on life. He realized he had no choice but to rely on himself and the tangible world around him. On the day of his medical school graduation, the President of Harvard University offered him the chance to become the founding chairman of the newly formed Department of Psychology. William welcomed the chance to turn his attention to the scientific study of the human mind—possibly as a way of getting some perspective on his own psychological troubles.

For a few years, James narrowed his investigations to neurophysiology. But the metaphysical curiosity elicited in his youth kept steering him to more exciting psychological topics. While reviewing a book titled *The Anaesthetic Revelation and the Gist of Philosophy*, he learned about the subjective effects of nitrous oxide gas. The book recounted the amateur philosopher Paul Blood's claim that breathing nitrous oxide triggered an immediate "insight of immemorial Mystery." Blood was convinced that he had stumbled upon a pharmacological pathway leading straight to spiritual enlightenment. He had experienced firsthand that all is in God and God is in all. The gist of his anaesthetic philosophy was thus quite simple: "The kingdom of God is ... within you; it is the Soul."[7]

James was a scientist. An idea is scientifically sound only to the extent that it is supported by experimental evidence. For this reason, James decided to inhale nitrous oxide and see for himself. The results were impressive. The intoxication proved so enjoyable that James was moved to "urge others to repeat the experiment, which with pure gas is short and harmless enough." He informed his readers that despite some personal variation, the subjective effects of nitrous oxide exhibit a general pattern: "With me, as with every other person of whom I have heard, the keynote of the experience is the tremendously exciting sense of an intense metaphysical illumination."[8]

This metaphysical illumination became the signal event in James's personal and professional life. Among other things, this illumination gave him confidence that he understood mystical experience from the mystic's own standpoint. About 20 years later, in 1902, he published what is probably the most famous academic study of religion ever produced, *The Varieties of Religious Experience*. Not surprisingly, *Varieties* argues that religion originates in personal, mystical experience. James explained that all of the various creeds and rituals associated with the world's religions are little more than secondhand translations of the original mystical experiences from which they arose. The core insight of mystical experience was that a wider spiritual universe exists at the furthest reaches of the human mind.

> Some years ago, I myself made some observations on this aspect of nitrous oxide intoxication, and reported them in print. One conclusion was forced upon my mind at that time, and my impression of its truth has ever since remained unshaken. It is that our normal waking consciousness, rational consciousness as we call it, is but one special type of consciousness, whilst all about it, parted from it by the filmiest of screens, there lie potential forms of consciousness entirely different.[9]

James acknowledged that our rational consciousness has utility in helping us adapt to the physical and social environments. But he urged us to consider how other states of consciousness (e.g., dreaming, hypnosis, mysticism) have their own utilities: "We may go through life without suspecting their existence; but apply the requisite stimulus, and at a touch they are there in all their completeness, definite types of mentality which probably, somewhere have their field of application and adaptation."[10] Indeed, James concluded, drug-induced illumination is but another avenue to the metaphysical truths of correspondence and influx.

> The whole drift of my education goes to persuade me that the world of our present consciousness is only one out of many worlds of consciousness that exist, and that those other worlds must contain experiences which have a meaning for our life also; and that although in the main their experiences and those of this world keep discrete, yet the two become continuous at certain points, and higher energies filter in.[11]

James's discovery of psychedelic illumination was soon to be replicated across Europe and North America. In 1943, a Swiss pharmaceutical researcher by the name of Albert Hofmann was studying alkaloids that might be valuable in obstetrics. His particular research specialty involved ergot alkaloids, which were produced by a fungus that grows on rye. He was working on his twenty-fifth variant of lysergic acid derivatives when he started to feel intoxicated. Many of his initial symptoms were unpleasant. Yet over the next few weeks, he continued to ingest microdoses of his LSD-25. It was, he discovered, a "sacred drug" in that it forges a mystical union between self and world:

> This condition of cosmic consciousness, which under favorable conditions can be evoked by LSD or by another hallucinogen from the group of Mexican sacred drugs, is analogous to spontaneous religious enlightenment, with the *unio mystica*. In both conditions, which often last only for a timeless moment, a reality is experienced that exposes a gleam of the transcendental reality, in which universe and self, sender and receiver, are one.[12]

The next few decades witnessed a steady stream of new converts to the psychedelic gospel. Thomas Huxley was an accomplished intellectual and author, as evidenced by his bestselling novel *Brave New World*. He had, furthermore, studied the mystical traditions of both Hinduism and Buddhism prior to publishing *Perennial Philosophy*. The basic thesis of his book on perennialism is that Asian mystics had developed pathways to experiencing the impersonal "One" that underlies the totality of existence. This background in metaphysical philosophy proved fortuitous when, in 1953, he ingested mescaline, which is the principal psychoactive agent found in the peyote cactus. Within minutes of ingesting the mescaline, Huxley reported that his visual perceptions were intensifying. Colors became brighter and more vivid. He soon noticed bright nodes of energy slowly dancing around a nearby vase of flowers. Moments later, he was beholding the universe in its indescribable glory. Huxley proclaimed that his mescaline-enhanced perception was that of "seeing what Adam had seen on the morning of his creation—the miracle, moment by moment, of naked existence." [13]

When trying to communicate his mescaline-induced epiphany, Huxley recalled a line from William Blake's *Marriage of Heaven and Hell*: "If the doors of perception were cleansed, everything would appear to man as it really is, infinite." Huxley proclaimed that mescaline had cleansed his doors of perception. Once the distortions imposed by our rational intellect were removed, Huxley could momentarily inhabit "a world where everything shone with Inner Light, and was infinite in its significance."[14]

Huxley's eloquent descriptions of psychedelic illumination became a clarion call for others eager to cleanse the doors of spiritual perception. Among the most famous to heed this call were Harvard psychologists Timothy Leary and Richard Alpert. Their Harvard Psychedelic Drug Research Project sought to "arrange transcendent experiences" by administering psychedelics to over 1,000 subjects. Among them were students, writers, artists, convicts, and 69 ordained clergy members. The most notable of these test subjects were Aldous Huxley, Allen Ginsberg, Alan Watts, and Huston Smith—all four of whom wrote eloquently about the experience and in doing so made explicit connections with other SBNR themes or interests.

Harvard warned Leary and Alpert not to use undergraduate students in their psychedelic sessions. They never complied.

Rumors of ribald partying and sexual dalliance in Leary's office swept across campus. Harvard officials had no recourse but to remove Leary and Alpert from the faculty and shut down their center for psychedelic research. Richard Alpert later relocated to India, where he took up the practice of yoga meditation and changed his name to Ram Dass. Dass continued to acknowledge psychedelics' value in helping people break out of their restricted consciousness. But he maintained that such an awakening is only the beginning of an authentic spiritual life. He shifted the focus of his SBNR advocacy to instructions on meditative practice.

Leary, however, was more determined than ever to advance the cause of psychedelics. He relied on the income generated by book royalties and speaking fees to fund his somewhat decadent lifestyle until his death in 1996. One of his continuing themes was that drugs such as mescaline and LSD led to the dissolution of the ego and in this way ushered people into the same transcendent states described by Hindu, Buddhist, and Daoist mystics. Several of his publications cited passages from Asian religious texts in order to explain the inner experience of psychedelic journeys. One of his earlier books, *Psychedelic Prayers*, freely cited the Chinese text *The Dao De Jing*. Leary, Dass, and Ralph Metzner co-authored a book titled *The Psychedelic Experience*, which attempted to explain the similarities between drug-driven illuminations and the mystic accounts contained in *The Tibetan Book of the Dead*. *The Tibetan Book of the Dead* is an ancient Buddhist text purporting to explain the realities (termed *bardos*) into which one travels following physical death. Leary's point was that psychedelic research had at long last uncovered the fundamental truths uniting East and West. This volume eventually went through 16 editions and was translated into seven languages. No matter how much controversy and bad publicity Leary generated during his decades-long career, he had long-lasting influence on how psychedelics would forever be embraced as a possible avenue to spiritual enlightenment.

Sociologist Wade Clark Roof tried to make sense of the spiritual journeys undertaken by the so-called Baby Boom generation. He interviewed a number of people in his effort to understand why so many in this generation left organized religion and yet remained intensely interested in spiritual topics. His interview with a woman by the name of Mollie provided him with one important clue. Mollie related that her spiritual journey began in the 1960s when she experimented with psychedelics. Roof reports that Mollie has been on a spiritual quest ever since. She has explored many of the spiritual and human potential alternatives of the post-1960s period: holistic health, macrobiotics, Zen Buddhism, Native American rituals, New Age in its many versions. She's read a lot about reincarnation and world religions.... She's an explorer down many paths.[15]

Much like William James before her, Mollie's drug-induced metaphysical illumination launched her on a journey defined by being SBNR. Along the way, she dabbled in Asian religions, metaphysical philosophies, Native American practices, and alternative medical systems. The bookstores she visited placed works about these topics in the same section, encouraging browsers to see the implicit metaphysical connections all these SBNR interests held in common. Mollie, like so many other Americans, displayed a talent for being "combinative" and piecing together her own SBNR profile. Psychedelics may have been her launching point, but Mollie traveled a spiritual path that brought her into contact with a good many of the same SBNR interests shared by countless others of her generation.

FEMINIST, LGBQT, AND ECOLOGICAL PERSPECTIVES

The rise of two important movements—the women's liberation movement and the Lesbian/Gay/Bi/Queer/Trans (LGBQT) movement—made increasing numbers of people receptive to becoming SBNR. It wasn't until the 1960s and 1970s that females gained any access to society's most powerful institutions. The medical, legal, and financial professions were slow to admit women into their ranks. This was true of religion, too. Even though women outnumbered men in virtually every religious organization in Europe or North America, men had a near-exclusive monopoly on the right to preach from the pulpit, teach in seminaries, or publish in theological journals. A few females tried to encourage institutional religion to find more important roles for women. They tried to show that the sexist customs, practices, and attitudes of ancient culture had influenced their religious institutions from the very beginning. They argued that it was now time to identify these sexist elements and adjust them in ways that would give women equal representation. These attempts to reform religious institutions from within were, however, typically ignored.

The most fascinating individual in the formation of feminist spiritualities is Mary Daly. She was born in Schenectady, New York, in 1928 and raised in a Roman Catholic family. A boy in her Catholic elementary school taunted her, bragging that he was an altar boy and that girls weren't allowed to serve Mass. This was only the first in a long line of similar experiences. The message was always the same: the doors of the church aren't—and never will be–open to women. After graduating from college, she found that there was not a single university in the country that would admit women to study Catholic theology at the doctoral level. She came across an advertisement for a newly opened School of Sacred Theology at St. Mary's College in Notre Dame, Indiana. The school's president not only admitted Mary Daly into the program but also offered her a scholarship that made it possible for her to earn a doctorate in philosophical theology by the age of 25.

Daly continued her theological education by earning two more doctorates at the University of Freiburg in Switzerland. In 1966, she was offered a position as professor of theology at Boston College, a Jesuit-run Catholic university with a reputation for having a liberal theological bent. Just two years later, she published her first book, *The Church and the Second Sex*. The book seems quite mild by today's cultural standards. But in 1968, it was perceived as an outright assault on the authority of the Roman Catholic church. Daly's main point in the book is that organized religion must finally reform those teachings that assign women the status of second-class citizens. She noted, for example, that Catholic doctrines about Mary envision the ideal woman as passive and self-sacrificing, finding fulfillment only through motherhood. Daly also drew attention to the sexist attitudes deeply embedded in Western conceptions of God. She argued that Christianity has persistently portrayed God as a Father, Christ as that Father's only Son, and all 12 apostles of that Son were also male. In sharp contrast to men, women can find no connection between their gender and divinity.

Mary Daly wasn't prepared for the strong reaction to her book. On the one hand, many female scholars and lay women enthusiastically embraced its arguments. But the male faculty and administration of Boston College thought otherwise. Daly was immediately fired. Nearly 1,500 students showed up for a campus demonstration in support of Daly's academic freedom. The controversy drew national media attention, and the college administration quietly reinstated her to the faculty. But Mary was forever changed. She had initially thought that there was a pure core at the center of Christianity that had unfortunately been corrupted by the sexist attitudes of ancient culture. She therefore believed these corrupting elements could be identified and eliminated. Her views on this had now changed. She became convinced that Christian teachings were oppressive to their very core. This realization signaled a new stage in her spiritual journey. Daly cut ties with the Catholic Church and set off alone to explore the possibilities of a feminist spirituality.

Daly's next book, *Beyond God the Father* (1973) challenged the way that organized religion identifies God as masculine. She showed her readers that images of a Father who art in Heaven have supported cruel and oppressive behavior for centuries. They have led to hierarchical political, social, and domestic practices that require subordination and oppression—enforced by violence whenever necessary. She argued that culture would be far better served by thinking of God in impersonal (gender neutral) or even feminist ways. Like Emerson, James, or other SBNR spokespersons, she often referred to God in metaphors of spiritual force or life-giving energy. She often referred to God as "Be-ing" and urged people—especially women—to adopt lifestyles that enable them to further the ongoing movement of Be-ing throughout the universe. Feminist spirituality, in her view, meant learning to cast off the limitations imposed on us by oppressive social institutions and cultivate the courage it takes to move our world to health and wholeness.

Daly, like all people who gravitate toward the SBNR outlook, found it easier to be clear about what she was against than what she was for. She stands out in the SBNR tradition, though, precisely because she worked tirelessly to think of ways to express her spirituality in a vocabulary that affirmed women's quest for fully expressing their innate potentials. Daly assured her readers that women's history contains a storehouse of woman-identified and woman-honoring spiritual symbols that they can appropriate in their own personal quests. Many of these come from the pagan traditions that Western institutional religion tried so hard to suppress. Other symbols come from women's historic concern with nurturing life all around them. Even domestic tasks, such as weaving, point to women's historic role in healing and connecting life rather than pulling it apart. Creating our own spiritual path requires "weaving world tapestries of our own kind. That is, about dis-covering, developing the complex web of living/loving relationships of our own kind. It is about women living, loving, creating our Selves, our cosmos."[16]

Daly was well aware that her relentless critiques of male-centered religion drew heavy criticism. Many church authorities called her a deviant. She didn't try to dodge such criticisms. Instead, she leaned into them. She noted that the beginning of liberation comes when women refuse to be "good" and/or "healthy" by prevailing standards. To be female is to be deviant by definition in the prevailing culture. To be female and defiant is to be intolerably deviant. This means going beyond the imposed definitions of "bad woman" and "good woman."

In a similar vein, she pointed out that the word "sin" is derived from the Indo-European root "es-," meaning "to be." Daly thus urged women to sin and sin big. She observed that women's newfound abilities to be—and to be big—might be our planet's only hope of shaking off the destructive effects that male-driven institutions have had on our natural environment.

At one point, Mary Daly became thoroughly exasperated with men's lack of sensitivity to women's quests for more opportunities. She coined the term "spiritual lesbianism" to capture her new conviction that women can't count on men for nurturance and must instead rely on other women. Daly's provocative phraseology draws attention to the fact that those who are lesbian, gay, bisexual, queer, or transgender have always experienced trauma in organized religion. Most institutional religions have historically labeled LGBQT individuals as deviant sinners. Most, too, adamantly exclude them from rituals such as marriage or ordination. It is thus easy to understand the ready affinity between LGBQT individuals and many expressions of alternative spirituality. SBNR viewpoints emphasize energy, inner peace, and creating stronger connections with yourself and loved ones. Rather than requiring confession of sins or subordination to authority as is common with institutional religion, SBNR viewpoints promote self-discovery and a celebration of life in all of its various expressions.

We might also note that long before Mary Daly began writing, there was a small cadre of women who had turned their back on institutional religion and instead embraced the Goddess tradition. Many identified themselves as witches. They used this term strategically, knowing full well that it elicited confused and negative reactions. They knew they were going across the grain of mainstream culture. Better, then, to challenge cultural biases head-on and invite audiences to stretch their own preconceptions about both gender and religion. Being a witch means not relying on male authorities to find ways of worshipping or connecting with the divine. Being a witch, instead, means seeking ritual practices that call forth the power-from-within.

Modern witches are a subset of the larger revival of pagan concepts. What we often call Neo-Paganism is a loosely associated cluster of small groups claiming to draw upon the religious imagery of premodern societies. Some studies suggest that there are over 250,00 Neo-Pagans in the United Kingdom and over a million in North America. These studies also show that their members tend to be young to middle-aged adults, mostly white urbanites, have a college degree, and by a slight majority, female. Pagans are, in other words, ordinary citizens of Western countries. The one thing they share in common is that they have rejected institutional religion and prefer forms of spirituality that emphasize the sacredness of nature. Most don't think that we can create a vision of a new culture unless we first change how we refer to the ultimate source of power—God. They point out that the biblical concept of God as a male authority figure is connected with centuries of sexism, racism, and ecological exploitation. As one modern neo-pagan explains, we need to find new ways of thinking about the divine energy that provides the "power from within" sustaining our universe.

> There are many names for power-from-within, none of them entirely satisfying. It can be called spirit—but that name implies that it is separate from matter.... It could be called God—but the God of patriarchal religions has been the ultimate source and repository of power-over. I have called it immanence, a term that is truthful but somewhat cold and intellectual. And I have called it Goddess, because the ancient images, symbols and myths of the Goddess, as birth-giver, weaver, earth and growing plant, wind and ocean, flame, web, moon and mild, all speak to me of the powers of connectedness, sustenance, and healing.[17]

Both feminist and LGBQT spiritualities overlap with ecological concerns. Those committed to "deep ecology" believe that it is not enough to create sustainable systems of agriculture, economics, and technology. They maintain that we also need a sustainable religion. As Carlene Spretnak explained in her *Spiritual Dimensions of Green Politics*, a sustainable spirituality is one that highlights "the true nature of being: all in One, all forms of existence comprise one continuous dance of matter/energy arising and falling away, arising and falling away."[18] What is more, Spretnak writes, a sustainable spirituality must awaken within us flashes of "God consciousness" which she equates with "awe at the intricate wonders of creation and celebration of the cosmic unfolding."[19]

Many of those attracted to an ecological spirituality cite James Lovelock's "Gaia hypothesis" that the Earth behaves as a single entity, a living Goddess. Still others link their holistic vision with the worldviews held by Native Americans and other indigenous peoples. It is, in fact, quite common for those drawn to SBNR viewpoints to romanticize Native American spirituality. A great deal of literature aimed at popular reading audiences extols Native American societies as rife with wisdom about how humans can live in harmony with nature. As a book on Native American perspectives on environmental justice touted, "Indian spiritual values, especially the attitude toward the Earth, may hold out a key to the survival of the planet and all its peoples."

A TRADITION OF COMBINATIVENESS

The world's major religions didn't appear out of nowhere. Their beliefs, rituals, and lifestyles developed over centuries, even millennia. Belonging to an institutional religion means thinking and behaving in ways shaped by these historical traditions.

Being SBNR also has a tradition (though its roots don't stretch back quite so far back in history). Being SBNR is thus to some extent about picking and choosing from among those beliefs, rituals, and lifestyles that have circulated among spiritual seekers over the course of several generations.

What most stands out in this brief survey of SBNR's beginnings is its penchant for combinativeness. Advocates of any one alternative spirituality mix and match vocabulary that might have first originated in quite different metaphysical systems. Bookstores display publications about alternative spiritual practices in the same section regardless of their very different origins. Anyone who comes to find a book about one specific tradition soon finds herself or himself browsing and discovering. Lectures, workshops, and even websites similarly link otherwise unconnected individuals into a loose-knit spiritual community.

Some curious people might simply be interested in finding an alternative medical treatment for a specific health problem. Yet in the act of learning about any one alternative medicine, newcomers quickly come across references to wide-ranging systems of "energy healing" and other metaphysical philosophies. Other curious people might be interested in recycling or renewable energy and then find themselves learning about deep ecology. And still others might be seeking to bolster their self-esteem and immerse themselves in human potential psychologies. In each and every case, newcomers will soon encounter references to a very similar mixture of unconventional philosophies: yoga, Transcendental Meditation, microdosing with psychedelics, neopagan ritual, hidden powers of the unconscious mind, Ye Jing, Zen, Therapeutic Touch, etc. Sustained exposure to even one of these alternative spiritualities guarantees at least some sense of recognition and affinity with many others. The SBNR movement has continued over the last two hundred years not by insisting on steadfast loyalty to a single creed—but by encouraging our tendency for combinativeness. Despite the existence of so many different "offbeat" philosophies, they somehow come together in the lives of their like-minded and like-hearted seekers.

NOTES

1 Abraham Maslow, *Toward a Psychology of Being* (Princeton, NJ: D. Van Nostrand Co., 1962), p. 333.
2 Abraham Maslow, *Toward a Psychology of Being* (Princeton, NJ: D. Van Nostrand Co., 1962), p. 277.
3 Abraham Maslow, *Religions, Values, and Peak Experiences* (New York, NY: Viking Press, 1970), p. 54.
4 Abraham Maslow, *Religions, Values, and Peak Experiences* (New York, NY: Viking Press, 1970), p. viii.
5 Abraham Maslow, *The Further Reaches of Human Nature* (New York, NY: Viking Press, 1972), p. 112.
6 R.M. Bucke, *Cosmic Consciousness* (New York, NY: Carol Publishing Group, 1993), p. 4.
7 A discussion of Blood's nitrous oxide-induced mystical philosophy can be found in Hal Bridges, *American Mysticism* (New York, NY: Harper & Row, 1970), pp. 15–19.
8 James's initial publication on nitrous oxide appeared in *Mind*, 7 (1882): 186–208. It also appears in an abridged form as "Subjective Effects of Nitrous Oxide," in Charles Tart, ed., *Altered States of Consciousness* (Garden City, NY: John Wiley & Sons, 1969), pp. 367–370.
9 William James, *The Varieties of Religious Experience* (Cambridge, MA: Harvard University Press, 1985), p. 307.

10 William James, *The Varieties of Religious Experience* (Cambridge, MA: Harvard University Press, 1985), p. 308.
11 William James, *The Varieties of Religious Experience* (Cambridge, MA: Harvard University Press, 1985), p. 408.
12 Albert Hofmann, *LSD: My Problem Child* (New York, NY: McGraw-Hill, 1980), p. 198.
13 Aldous Huxley, *The Doors of Perception* (San Francisco, CA: Harper & Row, 1954), p. 16.
14 Aldous Huxley, *The Doors of Perception* (San Francisco, CA: Harper & Row, 1954), p. 22.
15 Wade Clark Roof, *A Generation of Seekers: The Spiritual Journeys of the Baby Boom Generation* (San Francisco, CA: Harper, 1993), p. 22.
16 Mary Daly, *Gyn/Ecology: The Metaethics of Radical Feminism* (Boston, MA: Beacon Press, 1978), p. 10.
17 Starhawk, *Dreaming the Dark: Magic, Sex and Politics* (Boston, MA: Beacon Press, 1982), p. 4.
18 See Charlene Spretnak, *The Spiritual Dimension of Green Politics* (Santa Fe, NM: Bear, 1986), p. 41. An excellent overview of Spretnak's discussion of the spiritual dimensions of commitment to Green causes can be found in Catherine Albanese's *Nature Religion in America* (Chicago, IL: The University of Chicago Press, 1990), pp. 173–176.
19 Charlene Spretnak, *The Spiritual Dimension of Green Politics* (Santa Fe, NM: Bear, 1986), p. 42.

BIBLIOGRAPHY

Albanese, C. *Nature Religion in America*. Chicago, IL: The University of Chicago Press, 1990.

Bridges, H. *American Mysticism*. New York, NY: Harper & Row, 1970.

Bucke, R.M. *Cosmic Consciousness*. New York, NY: Carol Publishing Group, 1993.

Daly, M. *Beyond God the Father*. Boston, MA: Houghton Mifflin Co., 1973.

Daly, M. *Gyn/Ecology: The Metaethics of Radical Feminism*. Boston, MA: Beacon Press, 1978.

Hofmann, A. *LSD: My Problem Child*. New York, NY: McGraw-Hill, 1980.

Huxley, A. *The Doors of Perception*. San Francisco, CA: Harper & Row, 1954.

James, W. *The Varieties of Religious Experience*. Cambridge, MA: Harvard University Press, 1985.

Maslow, A. *Toward a Psychology of Being*. Princeton, NJ: D. Van Nostrand Co., 1962.

Maslow, A. *Religions, Values, and Peak Experiences*. New York, NY: Viking Press, 1970.
Maslow, A. *The Further Reaches of Human Nature*. New York, NY: Viking Press, 1972.
Mercadante, L. *Belief without Borders: Inside the Minds of the Spiritual but Not Religious*. New York, NY: Oxford University Press, 2014.
Parsons, W.B. *Freud and Religion: Advancing the Dialogue*. Cambridge, MA: Cambridge University Press, 2021.
Rieff, P. *The Triumph of the Therapeutic*. New York, NY: Harper, 1966.
Roof, W.C. *A Generation of Seekers: The Spiritual Journeys of the Baby Boom Generation*. San Francisco, CA: Harper, 1993.
Spretnak, C. *The Spiritual Dimension of Green Politics*. Santa Fe, NM: Bear, 1986.
Starhawk. *Dreaming the Dark: Magic, Sex and Politics*. Boston, MA: Beacon Press, 1982.

BEING SBNR

Beliefs, practices, personality profiles

We have traced the cultural strands that combined in ways that made being spiritual but not religious (SBNR) a viable form of modern spirituality. But what do we know about people who identify as SBNR today? What are their beliefs? What practices do they use to bring themselves into harmony with an unseen, divine reality? And why do some people embrace being SBNR more readily than other people?

We need to remember that those who identify as SBNR do so as a way of distinguishing themselves from people who consider adherents of an organized religious tradition ("conventionally religious"). This is the "not religious" part of being SBBR. But they also identify as SBNR as a way of distinguishing themselves from those who are wholly nonreligious. This is the "spiritual" part of being SBNR.

SBNR has become a viable option for people throughout Europe and North America. Polling shows that somewhere between 22% and 27% of Americans identify as SBNR, with the number of SBNR Canadians slightly higher. Across all the countries of Western Europe, the percentage of SBNRs is approximately 11% (though as high as 23% of all Europeans report believing in at least some nontraditional ideas about the supernatural and 19% report that they meditate).

Being conventionally religious is quite common in the United States. A full 62% of Americans claim at least some allegiance to a religious tradition. Weekly attendance at a formal worship service is about 38% in the United States. By contrast, being conventionally religious is less common in Europe,

DOI: 10.4324/9781003604259-4

where about 38% report allegiance to a religious tradition and weekly attendance is less than 10% in most Western European countries. Those leaning toward the SBNR outlook are first and foremost distinguishing themselves from their more religious counterparts.

Being wholly nonreligious is more common in Europe than in either the United States or Canada. Indeed, more than 60% of all adults in Western European countries such as Sweden, Norway, the Netherlands, Denmark, and Belgium claim to be neither religious nor spiritual. In the United States, only about 10% to 14% of adults tell pollsters that they are either atheist or agnostic, meaning that they are suspicious of belief in the supernatural. And, again, those leaning toward the SBNR outlook are also distinguishing themselves from their counterparts who embrace a more fully secular viewpoint.

So just what do people who describe themselves as SBNR stand for? What do they stand against? In what ways are they more like the nonreligious and in what ways are they more like the conventionally religious? What do we know about the personality traits of those who are SBNR? And how do those traits differ from the personalities of those who are either wholly nonreligious or who are conventionally religious? In sum, how can we characterize what it means to be SBNR?

SBNR BELIEFS/ATTITUDES

Being SBNR is defined by holding attitudes that differ from those who are wholly nonreligious (hence being in some way spiritual) and from those who are conventionally religious (hence not adhering to the beliefs or practices of organized religion). We can identify at least four of these attitudes that characterize what it means to be SBNR. Three of these attitudes separate SBNR individuals from those who are conventionally religious. The fourth attitude is what separates SBNR individuals from those who are wholly nonreligious. Together, these attitudes carve out a distinct "middle path" that promises to be the most viable approach to spirituality in the twenty-first century.

In making these comparisons, we must simplify our characterizations of what it means to "be religious" or "be nonreligious" to some extent. Surely some individuals who identify with either of these identities will think that these characterizations don't account for nuances or subtle shifts in emphasis. This will be particularly true of individuals belonging to liberal-leaning religious groups such as Reform Judaism or churches often characterized as mainline Protestant denominations. But, to be clear, these liberal-leaning groups have veered from their traditions' historical creeds and manner of reading scripture. These liberal-leaning groups have, moreover, created an ethos receptive to the very attitudes that distinguish being SBNR. Many of their members straddle these categories. Our intention here is to describe the attitudinal differences that—on the whole–distinguish what "being SBNR" means in contrast to being either conventionally religious or nonreligious. Some simplifications are inevitable.

The first attitude distinctive to being SBNR is to believe that it is not just the right—but even the duty—of individuals to decide what is true or not true for themselves. This attitude is shared by people who are wholly nonreligious. They, too, feel no pressure to accept beliefs simply "on faith." This SBNR attitude fits nicely in modern democratic societies that value individual rights, openly embrace pluralism, and advocate the separation of church and state.

This insistence on choosing for oneself is the attitude that most clearly separates being SBNR from being conventionally religious. Being religious has historically required pledging loyalty to the group's signature belief system. Attendance at a weekly worship service usually entails standing and collectively reciting statements of shared religious belief. Religions typically urge members not to succumb to doubts of any kind. It is true that some liberal-leaning Christian and Jewish congregations embrace some element of doubt, but historically, most members of a Western religious community are warned to shun even the slightest hint of doubt. Indeed, conservative religious groups often claim that the Devil is trying to lure people away from God and does so by planting seeds of doubt that will lead them away from the narrow path of faith. Believers are warned about the consequences of questioning religious authority: social disapproval in this life and eternal damnation upon death.

Existentially speaking, BSBNR requires some courage. It means giving up the comfort of total certainty. It means being willing to face up to some doubts and some uncertainty. It means risking disapproval from family, friends, and neighbors.

Deciding for oneself does, however, brings its own kinds of emotional comfort. Pretending to believe takes a lot of effort. Finding the courage to speak in one's own voice brings relief. It also brings a sense of authenticity.

Those who opt for the SBNR stance toward personal religiosity do not expect to find the kind of fixed, absolute truths at the core of organized religion. They often speak of being on a spiritual journey rather than of having found a permanent religious dwelling. The sociologist Robert Wuthnow found it convenient to refer to conventionally religious individuals as "dwellers." Being SBNR, he explains, is about choosing to be a "seeker" and continually changing one's views in light of going experience.[1] Seekers forego the security and certainty of a stable religious shelter. They rarely expect to find absolute truths, but instead seek provisional truths; that is, they explore religious ideas and experiment with them to determine how well these ideas fit with their overall personal experience.

Most SBNR seekers don't expect religion to be about truth at all, if by truth we mean the kind of verifiable facts found in natural science or mathematics. One of the leading Transcendentalists, George Ripley, stated that "the truth of religion does not depend on tradition nor historical facts, but has an unerring witness in the soul." By this, Ripley meant that the "truth" of religion is about each of us opening ourselves to an encounter with an order of existence "which transcends the external senses."[2] The final test of religious truth thus has nothing to do with ancient beliefs or dogmas. It is about our own spiritual feelings and judgments.

A second attitude that characterizes what it means to be SBNR is **skepticism toward organized religion.** This attitude is also shared by those who adopt the wholly nonreligious viewpoint. Both groups report that they don't rely on organized religion to find meaning in their lives or to choose between right and wrong. Both groups—the nonreligious and the SBNR—are twice as likely as their conventionally religious counterparts to think that organized religion does more harm than good. Being SBNR is, at least in part, about finding organized religion problematic.

We might remember that Ralph Waldo Emerson was an ordained minister and chose to leave religion precisely because he found Sunday morning worship services to be dull and boring. Many of those who opt for being SBNR agree that organized religion strikes them as emotionally cold. Many, however, cite far more negative experiences with organized religion than just finding it dull and boring. Some point out that biblical religion is out of touch with a world defined by scientific discoveries. For centuries, the Church has attacked science (from Galileo's assertion that the earth revolves around the sun to Darwin's assertions about the biological origins of the human species). Religion has always been wrong. Others point to the utter hypocrisy of church leaders who so often live immoral lives in private while condemning such behavior in public. Still others point to the belittling and emotional suffering they have personally experienced at the hands of church leaders. This might mean being ignored simply for one's gender. It might also mean being openly condemned for one's gender or sexual identity. And it might even mean having been the victim of sexual abuse. Similarly, many of those who embrace being SBNR believe that religion has historically served to perpetuate the interests of the ruling class. Religion, it seems, functions in ways that encourage submissiveness and obedience to morally corrupt social structures (e.g., racism, economic disparities, sexism, imperialism, etc.).

A **third attitude** that demarcates the SBNR identity is its view that **religion should not be about procuring an invisible afterlife; instead, religion should be about enriching this life.** Wholly nonreligious people share this attitude with those who are SBNR, too. This third SBNR attitude, however, contrasts sharply with conventional religiosity. Anthropologists have shown how religion emerged in human societies as a way of coaxing individuals to sacrifice their personal interests for the good of the group. A principal way of doing this was to create mythic stories suggesting that an all-seeing deity was monitoring our every behavior. Western religions preach that this deity is aware of our every thought or behavior. We are told that all good behavior will be rewarded and all bad behavior will be punished if not in this life, then certainly upon death (heavenly paradise vs. hell). Religion thereby instills a sufficient amount of fear about the possibility of eternal punishment as to motivate behavior deemed in the interests of society and its most powerful leaders.

This difference between focusing on the afterlife vs. focusing on this life is not absolute. It is more a matter of tone or emphasis. After all, traditional religions minister to the daily lives of their congregants. The Bible contains whole sections of "wisdom literature" that offer insights about how we might best navigate our way through the vicissitudes of daily living. Various forms of pastoral care and counseling help members apply biblical teachings to everyday life. Nonetheless, the historical core of Christianity is proclaiming the resurrection of Christ, which made eternal life possible for all sincere believers. The principal focus of Judaism has varied over the centuries, but surely most adherents have believed that some kind of afterlife reward awaits those who have followed the lifestyle outlined in scripture. The point here is that the motivation for adhering to Western religions has historically revolved around the hope of obtaining an eternal reward.

The majority of those who adopt the SBNR stance do believe that there is something about humans that transcends the physical body—a *spirit or soul* of some kind. And the majority believe that this soul or metaphysical essence survives physical death. There is no single view about the afterlife, but almost all embrace some—though often vague—belief that something positive awaits us upon death. Some entertain the notion of reincarnation adopted from Asian religions. They tend to view reincarnation, however, not so much in the Hindu fashion of threatening a miserable future for those who violate social norms. Instead, reincarnation is typically thought of as promising future opportunities for ongoing spiritual growth. Probably most of those who embrace being SBNR believe in some version of Western religion's heaven, where we might be reunited with friends and loved ones. What is rarely found in SBNR writings is any reference to hell. Being SBNR, it seems, is about emphasizing opportunities for future spiritual growth and refusing to entertain notions of eternal punishment.

SBNR's tendency to view spirituality as an approach to vibrant living is reflected in its range of *beliefs about God*. In sharp contrast to the agnostics and atheists who comprise the "wholly nonreligious" category, being SBNR includes belief in God. This belief in God, however, differs a great deal from the beliefs about God held by those who adhere to traditional, church-centered religion. We might, for example, remind ourselves that Christianity has traditionally proclaimed that God has three differing expressions as Father, Son, and Holy Spirit (the doctrine of the Holy Trinity). In contrast, SBNR views of God typically ignore notions of God as Father or Son. SBNR focuses instead solely on God as a spiritual force bringing vitality to the natural universe. Absent, of course, are conceptions of God as constantly judging humans and finding each and every one of us sinful. Absent, too, are conceptions of God incarnating as Jesus to be the one exception to this otherwise universal rule that humans are wretched sinners.

SBNR's revised concepts of God simultaneously change how it conceptualizes human nature. This includes changes in how it understands the word "sin." All three Western religions (Judaism, Christianity, and Islam) place sin at the center of their conceptions of human nature and humanity's relationship to God. All three religions claim that humans have fallen out of harmony with God on account of disobedience to his commands. This is the essence of the story about Adam and Eve in the Garden of Eden. The first humans disobeyed the commands of their Heavenly Father, and humanity has ever since been characterized by the condition of sin. In the SBNR approach, however, sin is not the condition of having disobeyed a Heavenly Father. Sin is instead interpreted as the condition of not having sufficiently opened oneself to the inflow of divine spiritual power. In the SBNR view, sin is simply estrangement from our own spiritual depths

Western religion has traditionally taught that we are dependent on male clergy members to mediate between us and God. We must look to preachers, priests, rabbis, or imams if we hope to be forgiven for our sinful disobedience. Being

SBNR, however, means striving to overcome this estrangement through our own efforts. Spiritual practices ranging from meditation to immersion in nature are intended to help us become inwardly receptive to an ever-available divine presence. As Emerson described spiritual awakening in his famous essay, *Nature*: "All mean egotism vanishes.... I am nothing; I see all; the currents of the Universal Being circulate through me; I am part and parcel of God."[3] Emerson—like most of those who are inclined toward being SBNR—understood full well that this new conception of sin makes Christianity's traditional teachings about Jesus irrelevant. To most of those who embrace being SBNR, Jesus is not the great exception to humanity, but rather the greatest example of what humanity might become insofar as we make an inward connection with divine inflow. Emerson's point was that in proclaiming Jesus' divinity, Christianity had lost sight of every human being's inner connection with the currents of Universal Being. Christianity attributes divine nature to Jesus, but denies it to the rest of us. In so doing, it loses any real sense of the spiritual inspiration that we are all capable to achieve. Similarly, the church speaks of miracles in the distant past, but has become blind to the higher spiritual power available to all of us in the here and now. The churches have in this sense become the enemy of authentic spirituality; they divert our attention from the miraculous possibilities of everyday human experience.

The **fourth attitude** expressed by those who embrace being SBNR is its **fascination with metaphysical experiences and realities.** The first three attitudes characterizing the SBNR outlook might be shared by those who are wholly nonreligious. This final attitude, however, identifies SBNR's explicitly spiritual orientation. Being SBNR is first and foremost about wanting a felt connection with more-than-physical dimensions of the universe. People who are wholly nonreligious utilize analytical reasoning in ways that exclude ideas that cannot be verified by the five physical senses. The cognitive style associated with being nonreligious thus systematically denies the more-than-physical (supernatural) realities affirmed both by conventionally religious and by SBNR individuals.

This penchant for believing in—and even experiencing—metaphysical realities is something that being SBNR shares with those who are conventionally religious. Being religious, however, means limiting one's conceptions of metaphysical realities to biblical teachings. Religious institutions channel their members' metaphysical proclivities toward a fairly narrow range of approved supernatural topics: a heavenly God, saints, and the various spiritual beings (e.g., angels) depicted in scripture. Being SBNR, however, is less constrained. Metaphysical curiosity launches seekers on an almost endless journey through the many metaphysical systems existing outside our churched traditions. Along these journeys, SBNR seekers will eventually encounter any number of metaphysical beliefs (auras, Ascended Masters, *chakras*, subtle body energies, etheric and astral realms, *qi*, spirit communication, parapsychological abilities) and metaphysical practices (meditation, use of crystal stones, seances, psychedelics, sensory deprivation, massage to activate subtle body energies).

Being SBNR includes some philosophical tension with both the views held by the conventionally religious and the views of those who are wholly nonreligious. Being SBNR means being curious about many kinds of metaphysical realities—most of which are condemned as heresies by biblically based religious groups. Those who are SBNR certainly do believe in the methods and findings of science, but they diverge from the nonreligious viewpoint insofar as they do not think that science is able to explore the most fascinating dimensions of existence. Being SBNR thus includes some tension with science and the scientific method. The philosopher/psychologist William James best described this fascination with metaphysical realities when he confessed that he had an obsession for what he called "searching for white crows." James was a scientist and thus fully embraced the scientific method. But he was utterly convinced that there was more to the universe than could be detected through conventional scientific methods. He wanted to prove this. All he needed to do was find at least one paranormal event that couldn't be explained according to known scientific laws. As he reasoned, "If you wish to upset the law that all crows are black, you mustn't seek to show that no crows are; it is enough if you prove one single crow to be white."[4] James, as with so many SBNRs after his time, was highly motivated to find at least one genuinely paranormal event. Just one truly metaphysical event might provide a solid foundation for a new spiritual understanding of the universe.

William James, incidentally, believed he found at least two such white crows. One of these was his certainty that a spiritualist medium by the name of Leonora Piper was able to discern information in ways that could not be explained by any scientifically trained psychologist. He also believed that the subjective experiences triggered by nitrous oxide provided first-hand evidence of a vast spiritual reality. White crows like these proved to James that there are resources in us that [science] never reckons of, possibilities that take our breath away, of another kind of happiness and power, based on giving up our own will and letting something higher work for us, and these seem to show a world wider than [the physical sciences] can imagine.[5]

The term "being spiritual" needs to mean something specific, or it becomes so vague as to be meaningless. It needs to mean something more than just being emotionally calm or feeling contented. What is unique to "being spiritual" is valuing efforts to connect with something that is more-than-physical. SBNR individuals share this attitude with conventionally religious individuals. Both groups desire to feel connected with realities that lie beyond the grasp of the physical senses. Conventionally religious people have had this spiritual inclination channeled to shared conceptions of these metaphysical realities. They envision the existence of a Father-like God, Christ, saints, an afterlife heaven, etc. SBNR individuals, on the other hand, have opted to explore metaphysical realities more widely. Their inclination to believe in—and seek connection with—metaphysical realities might lead them toward any number of alternative spiritual beliefs.

Recent studies of SBNR individuals across both North America and Europe find that they are highly likely to believe that humans have some kind of spirit or soul in addition to the physical body; to believe in astrology; to believe that the physical world contains spiritual energies (e.g., auras, *chakras*, *kundalini*, *prana*, *qi*, animal magnetism) not recognized by science; to believe in reincarnation; to believe that yoga is a spiritual practice, not just exercise; to meditate; and to consult horoscopes or other fortune-telling practices. All of these beliefs are distinctively spiritual in that they presuppose the same overarching attitude: that our greatest good comes from inwardly connecting with more-than-physical realities.

SBNR PRACTICES

Tradition-, institution-centered religiosity includes very specific practices: attending formal worship services, sitting/standing/kneeling behaviors, singing, reading from texts outlining professing faith, praying together with fellow believers, praying alone, reading scripture, donating money and/or time, participating in sacraments (e.g., confession, baptism, confirmation, marriage), etc. These practices bring a sense of serenity and fulfillment. They provide continuity and support on a regular basis, even as our personal lives go through various kinds of upheavals. By ritualizing the practice of religion, churches enact people's shared desire to find inner peace through the worship of their Heavenly Father.

Those who become SBNR, however, lack confidence in ceremonial worship. This is often because they have ceased believing in the kind of god who demands obedience or worship. They might also have found ceremonial worship boring and lifeless. Much like Ralph Waldo Emerson in the early 1800s, they drift away from the churches not because they seek less contact with the divine but because they seek more intense, deeply felt experiences of a sacred reality.

Being SBNR means valuing practices that inwardly open us to the inflow of higher power. Typically, however, they are not performed in public settings or at precise times or days of the week. The practice of being SBNR is what we might call *ad hoc* in nature, using the Latin phrase meaning "for this" or "for this only" rather than being part of a more generalized system of behaviors. Those drawn to being SBNR typically engage in spiritual behaviors on an *ad hoc* basis as their physical and emotional lives dictate: when sick, when grieving, when confused, when in need of inspiration, when facing economic difficulties, or when celebrating. It might help to compare SBNR practices to the way we listen to music. We don't typically listen to the same music every week at the same exact time, on the same exact day, and in the same exact location. Instead, we seek out a specific musical artist or musical genre to fit a specific mood or activity. The same with being SBNR. Being SBNR means seeking out specific spiritual practices to match changing moods and life events.

Being SBNR means being drawn to practices that inwardly open ourselves to the inflow of higher power. At heart, the SBNR practice hasn't changed much since the metaphysical systems that appeared throughout the nineteenth century. SBNR practices are predicated on the belief that the universe extends far beyond what can be detected by the physical senses. The key to spirituality, then, is establishing some kind of inner harmony or connection with these higher metaphysical realities. Achieving this harmony or connection makes possible the inflow of spiritual energies responsible for physical health, emotional well-being, and almost every kind of worldly prosperity.

Along these lines, we might remember how Emerson found that **walking silently in nature** helped him become inwardly receptive to sensations of divine inflow. This continues to be the most common practice associated with being SBNR. Indeed, almost one in four Americans report that they regularly seek opportunities to spend time in nature not simply for physical recreation but as a means of connecting with something bigger than themselves. Importantly, humans often experience profound moments of awe or wonder when suddenly surrounded by something bigger or vaster than ourselves. Awe and wonder cause us to feel small or insignificant—diminishing our everyday sense of self-importance. Awe and wonder are, for this reason, quintessentially spiritual emotions. They lure us into becoming receptive and to be drawn out toward a much wider universe. In these wonder-driven moments, we feel intimately connected with a universe that is valuable in and of itself independent of any usefulness to humans. In Emerson's own words, "all mean egotism vanishes. I become a transparent eyeball; I am nothing; I see all; the currents of the Universal Being circulate through me; I am part or parcel of God." Thick forests, mountain vistas, ocean panoramas, or vivid sunsets can all elicit these wonder-driven moments of connection with a wider sacred universe.

Meditating is probably the second most common practice associated with being SBNR. One form of meditation is called mindfulness. Mindfulness meditation only requires that we sit quietly and focus solely on our breathing in an effort to be fully aware of the present moment without the mind being distracted or wandering. Mindfulness brings composure and a feeling of being removed from the push and pull of public opinion. It also makes us aware of the sacredness of the here and now of everyday life. Some of those drawn to being SBNR learn to sit in Asian-style meditative positions developed in the practice of Hindu yoga or differing forms of Buddhist meditation. These meditative practices typically aim for cultivating inner-receptivity to higher metaphysical realities. Asian-born meditation practices have been a strong part of Western SBNR traditions for at least two hundred years, but they became especially prominent in the 1960s and 1970s when the psychedelic movement popularized highly spiritual interpretations of attaining altered states of consciousness.

Various **psycho-spiritualities** also provide practices for many in the SBNR category. Rather than spending time in a church listening to a sermon, the typical SBNRer is more likely to think about the meaning of their dreams or decide to go on a psychologically informed weekend retreat. Their goal might be described as "self-actualization," "personal authenticity," or attaining "peak experiences." But the common denominator is that they are cultivating their own capacity to connect inwardly with higher, divine energies.

Being SBNR often includes **various forms of body work**. SBNR's fascination with metaphysical realities includes a strong interest in the possibility that our bodies can become receptive to the inflow of subtle spiritual energies. Different metaphysical systems refer to these subtle energies by various names: *qi*, animal magnetism, *prana*, Innate, *kundalini*, energies flowing from our etheric or astral bodies. The ancient

Chinese practices of Tai Chi and Qigong are examples of spiritual body work designed to enhance the flow of metaphysical energy throughout our bodies. So, too, are many forms of massage, ranging from the Japanese system of Reiki, similarly thought to restore the flow of subtle spiritual energies. Yoga, while on the one hand considered by SBNR enthusiasts for its ability to evoke spiritual states of consciousness, is also renowned for restoring the body to a pristine state of natural health. What would distinguish a form of physical exercise or massage as spiritual, however, would be the intention of cultivating the inflow of subtle metaphysical energies into our physical bodies.

Often overlooked in surveys of SBNR spirituality is the **widespread popularity of divination practices such as astrology**. Being SBNR very much includes curiosity about the unseen forces affecting our lives. Divination practices offer one way of exploring what these forces might be and how we might accordingly adjust our thoughts or behaviors. Divination practices have historically included such "fortune-telling" systems as reading tea leaves, rune casting, numerology, or finding significance in special numbers, reading lines in the palms of our hands, the Chinese Yi Jing, divining or "witching" rods, Tarot cards, and Ouji boards. At least 30% of American adults tell pollsters that they consider astrology and other divination practices to be an important part of their daily lives.

SBNR individuals, much like their conventionally religious counterparts, like to **sit quietly in specific physical settings and to surround themselves with specific kinds of physical objects** in their ongoing effort to feel connected with a higher reality. Those who identify as Jewish might place a mezuzah or menorah in their home to signify their faith commitment. Christians similarly place Bibles, crosses, or figurines of either Jesus or Mary in their homes as a devotional practice. SBNR drawn to being SBNR often come from these backgrounds, and they, too, might have a cross or menorah placed prominently on a shelf or table. And just as conventionally religious individuals might have an altar or specially designated area for prayer, SBNR individuals might also create an altar or set aside a special spot in their homes for spiritual reading or meditation.

The metaphysical systems comprising SBNR history have often explained that crystals have a special ability to capacitate subtle spiritual energies. Thus, owning crystals or even meditating while holding a crystal in one's hands is a fairly common method of practicing alternative spirituality. Another practice expressing spiritual interests is wearing particular kinds of jewelry or having specific images or scriptural passages tattooed on one's body. Many Christians, for example, own specially selected jewelry (e.g., a cross necklace) to denote their religious desires. Other Christians adorn themselves with tattoos depicting religious icons or especially selected Bible verses. SBNR individuals, too, wear jewelry or display tattoos that commemorate their spiritual journeys.

SBNR practices express the movement's penchant for combinativeness. A sociological study of contemporary spirituality included an interview with a 38-year-old teacher living in the American Southwest.[6] She was raised Roman Catholic but now attends Mass only a few times a year. Despite her loss of interest in church-based religion, she still considers herself a spiritual person. She sets aside an hour every day for meditation. She has a home altar that symbolizes her personal spiritual beliefs. On this altar are 18 candles, an amulet attached to a photo of her grandmother, amethyst crystals used in healing meditations, oriental incense, a Tibetan prayer bell, a representation of the Virgin of Guadalupe, and some other traditional Catholic items. What stands out in all of this is that there is no clear separation between aspects of her Catholic upbringing (e.g., Virgin of Guadalupe) and aspects of her seeker spirituality (e.g., crystals and a Tibetan prayer bell). They combine seamlessly in her own spiritual journey.

CHARACTERIZING THOSE DRAWN TO SBNR

For much of the past two hundred years, being SBNR was associated with White males who were either middle or upper class and quite well educated. This association made sense. Higher levels of education and income gave them more leisure time and more opportunities to come across alternative religious philosophies. They were freer from socioeconomic stress and hence freer to experiment with ideas that risked some social disapproval. Even though people from all socioeconomic backgrounds quietly combined religious ideas in ways that made sense in their personal lives, more highly educated males were able to do so in a more systematic way.

Most of this is changing now. A recent survey in the United States observed that the trend toward identifying oneself as SBNR can now be found in all regions of the country and many demographic groups. While the drop in Christian affiliation is particularly pronounced among young adults, it is occurring among Americans of all ages. The same trends are seen among whites, blacks, and Latinos; among both college graduates and adults with only a high school education; and among women as well as men.[7]

An intriguing question remains. Why are some of us drawn to being SBNR? That is, why do some of us opt for being SBNR, rather than being conventionally religious or being wholly nonreligious?

We might ask, then, can academic psychology tell us anything about why people tend toward being SBNR? After all, the purpose of academic psychology is to explain why humans think, feel, or behave in the way we do. Psychology should, therefore, be able to shed some light on how we differ from one another in the way we approach religion or spirituality. This topic can get complicated, and academic psychology uses a lot of terminology that takes a long time to decipher. But there are a few key ideas that go a long way toward explaining the personality traits that predispose us toward being religious, being nonreligious, or being SBNR.[8]

A starting point is the psychological measure of the degree to which we approach life from our own individual standpoint (Individualism) or from the standpoint of the social groups to which we belong, such as our family or our tribe (Collectivism). People who measure higher in individualism are more likely to become either SBNR or wholly nonreligious than people who measure lower in individualism. People who measure higher in Collectivism are more likely to become conventionally religious. This is really not surprising. Being conventionally religious is very much about aligning oneself with the larger group's beliefs and practices. Conversely, being either SBNR or nonreligious is about being a nonconformer. On this psychological measure, then, individuals who naturally gravitate toward being SBNR share more in common with nonreligious people than they do with religious people.

A second approach to identifying characteristics of people who opt for being SBNR is describing their basic personality traits. Psychologists are in general agreement that we can be distinguished from one another according to five basic personality traits. These traits, commonly referred to as the Big Five, are (1) openness to experience (inventive/curious vs. consistent/cautious); (2) conscientiousness (efficient/complies with expectations vs. careless/less reliable); (3) extraversion (outgoing/energetic vs. solitary/reserved); (4) agreeableness (friendly/cooperative vs. judgmental/less cooperative); and (5) emotional instability (sensitive/nervous vs. resilient/confident). All of the Big Five personality traits correlate with our tendency to be religious/spiritual. But three of them—openness to experience, agreeableness, and conscientiousness—have the clearest relevance to identifying the traits most characteristic of those most likely to become SBBR.

Openness to experience is, among other things, a measure of our willingness to experiment and to investigate new ideas or life experiences. Both nonreligious and SBNR individuals tend to measure high in openness to experience. Conventionally religious individuals, on the other hand, tend to measure low in openness to experience.

As might be expected, high measures of both conscientiousness and agreeableness are strongly correlated with being conventionally religious. They both reflect an individual's predisposition to adjust her/himself to others. Both nonreligious and SBNR individuals tend to be lower in these traits of conscientiousness and agreeableness.

Thus far, we have noted that being SBNR is correlated with psychological measures of Individualism (vs. Collectivism) and with higher measures of openness to experience. It is easy to see how these psychological traits might explain why being SBNR and being nonreligious are characterized by three of the four "attitudes" toward religion we outlined above. Higher individualism and higher openness predispose us to seek out our own path even if it departs from traditional social viewpoints. Both of these traits, then, play a role in wanting to decide what is true for ourselves, for being wary of organized religion, and for thinking of spirituality more in terms of how it enhances this life rather than procuring an afterlife.

We have noted, however, that there is one important attitude—fascination with supernatural or metaphysical realities—that SBNR individuals share with those who are conventionally religious (but not with the nonreligious). The branch of psychology known as cognitive science is especially helpful in understanding why both of these groups believe in more-than-physical realities, even though many in our culture reject such beliefs altogether. The key insight, according to cognitive science, is that both SBNR and conventionally religious individuals have a psychological preference for intuitive rather than analytical thinking.

Cognitive science reminds us that the human brain is a physical organ. Like all other organs in our body, our brains are the final product of a long evolutionary history driven by genetic mutations and natural selection. Natural selection didn't design our brains to know cosmic truth. They were designed to guide efficient behavior. The sole purpose of all the kinds of perception and cognition that go on in our brains is to help us successfully interact with our physical and social surroundings. Most cognitive activity in our brains is automatic and spontaneous. We are rarely conscious of the brain's role in scanning our environments, selecting relevant information, and shaping this information in ways that ensure our biological safety. We breathe, digest food, fight off infections, and execute habitual behaviors with no deliberate mental effort. In this sense, most cognition happens naturally or intuitively without any conscious awareness. Our "intuitive" thinking happens so automatically and spontaneously that it just feels right to us.

We might once again note that evolution shaped intuitive thinking to guide efficient behavior, not to discover abstract philosophical, mathematical, or scientific truths. In fact, our intuitive cognition easily leads us toward religious (i.e., believing that events were caused by invisible beings) rather than scientific understandings of events. These automatic brain activities naturally and spontaneously assume that there are beings or energies separate from physical reality (what we call "dualism" in that they assume the existence of an invisible mind/spirit separate from the physical body). These brain functions also attribute human-like intentions to nonhuman events (what we call "anthropomorphism") in ways that make it natural to believe in spirit beings who can either help or hurt us. And, too, when our analytic reasoning is subdued and our intuitive cognition predominates, we often lose any sense of being a distinct, separate self and instead feel more connected to our surroundings. In other words, when our intuitive thinking is more prominent, we more easily feel a sense of connection to a wider universe. And studies show that individuals who gravitate toward being SBNR tend to rely more on intuitive than analytic modes of thinking.

Analytic reason, on the other hand, requires deliberate effort and sustained attention. Analytic reasoning is guided by information we have acquired through experience or education. It is alert to the role that coincidence or even self-deception might play when we try to understand suddenly occurring events. It employs reason and analysis. For these reasons, analytic reasoning tends to undermine the credibility of supernatural or metaphysical concepts—leading us toward a more scientific or nonreligious understanding of our world.

This additional psychological insight—our varying tendency to rely on either intuitive or analytic styles of cognition—goes a long way toward explaining why even people who stray away from organized religion are nonetheless highly drawn toward metaphysical beliefs. We know that nonreligious individuals measure higher in their reliance on analytic reasoning. We also know that both conventionally religious and SBNR individuals measure higher in their reliance on intuitive reasoning. These individuals trust and value their immediate cognitive understandings, which just feel right despite lacking in intellectual or scientific rigor. They intuitively think in dualistic (believing that the mind/spirit is separate from the body) and anthropomorphic (attributing thought or intentionality to nonhuman objects) ways—making supernatural or metaphysical belief seem natural. They also feel deeply connected with the wider universe in ways that support metaphysical understandings of ourselves and the world we live in.

SBNR individuals share many psychological traits with nonreligious individuals. But this last trait—heavy reliance on intuitive ways of knowing—is what makes them think and feel in spiritual ways. We might ask one final question: why do those who opt for being SBNR value intuitive understandings of the world more than their nonreligious counterparts? This is an interesting question because they typically have the same level of intelligence and education (both factors that ordinarily make people less likely to believe in supernatural or metaphysical ideas). There are at least three possible reasons why these individuals think so intuitively. The first possible reason is that, like every other human trait, our biological and social backgrounds reinforce this tendency. Every human trait is influenced by genetic factors. Even within the same family, there are going to be differences in our cognitive approach to life. Added to this, our families and peer groups differ in the degree to which they reinforce our differing cognitive tendencies. A second possible reason is that persons who end up embracing the SBNR outlook have experienced more positive emotions, such as awe and wonder. Vivid moments of wonder exert powerful influences on our cognition and perception. There is strong evidence that they increase our degree of openness to experience, create vivid sensations of being connected to a vaster reality, and trigger curiosity about unseen powers influencing our world. In short, individuals who have had vivid experiences of wonder become emotionally disposed to valuing their intuitive sense of the surrounding world. Finally, a third possible reason that individuals might gravitate toward intuitive ways of thinking is having experienced one or more altered states of consciousness, such as might be induced by meditation or certain mind-altering chemicals. Both meditative and psychedelic states of consciousness dismantle our normal sense of self.

By doing this, they also dismantle our usual sense of being distanced or separated from our surrounding world. As a result, they yield dramatic sensations of connection with the world around us. They make intuitive understandings of ourselves and the world we live in much more intense and convincing than what we know through analytic reasoning. Hence, experiencing altered states of consciousness, much like experiencing vivid moments of wonder, might affect the psychological factors that would predispose us to the distinctively SBNR fascination with metaphysical realities.

CARL JUNG'S INDIVIDUATION

The life of Carl Jung neatly illustrates this connection between personal traits and tendencies to embrace being SBNR. In the previous chapter, we saw that Jung was one of the pioneers of psycho-spirituality. His theory about human nature and his subsequent views on religion and spirituality became core elements of Jungian therapy and were included in the curriculum of the many Jung Institutes located around the world. These institutes function as an SBNR social space; one that is centered on the individual, is pluralistic, unchurched, spiritual, and therapeutic at the same time.

Jung (1875–1961) was born into a Protestant family in Switzerland. His father was a Protestant pastor. In that era, sons often followed the career choice of their father. Jung's interest in religion was apparent as a child, and he would often ask his father about difficult concepts like the nature of the Holy Trinity. Jung's father was vague in his answers and, in general, did little to encourage Carl to follow in his career footsteps. This initial inability to connect with his father's religion was exacerbated by subsequent events in young Carl's life. Two such events are catalogued in his spiritual autobiography titled *Memories, Dreams, Reflections*. The first event can be called the Cathedral fantasy. Jung describes a period in his youth where he was haunted by what he characterized as a blasphemous thought, deserving of eternal damnation, which was ignited by the sight of a beautiful cathedral in the town square. After repressing the thought for some time, he finally summoned the courage to let it come fully into consciousness:

> I gathered all my courage, as though I were about to leap forthwith into hell-fire, and let the thought come. I saw before me the cathedral, the blue sky. God sits on His golden throne, high above the world – and from under the throne an enormous turd falls upon the sparkling new roof, shatters it, and breaks the walls of the cathedral asunder. So that was it! I felt an enormous, an indescribable relief. Instead of the expected damnation, grace had come upon me ... [my father] did not know the immediate living God who stands, omnipotent and free, above His Bible and His Church.[9]

Psychologically speaking, this is an instance of "de-idealization." In order to believe any religious doctrine or institution, one must idealize it as being true. In this sense, idealization can be called the "developmental infrastructure" of belief. The two go hand-in-hand. But young Carl's Cathedral fantasy was the opposite. It showed a de-idealization of traditional religion in favor of a more unchurched, generic spirituality which admitted of a divine being outside church and tradition. The Cathedral experience was followed by another, equally disillusioning experience. Carl was approaching the day of his confirmation into church membership. He had completed the long course of religious education, and the big day came:

> Suddenly my turn came. I ate the bread; it tasted flat, as I had expected. The wine, of which I took only the smallest sip, was thin and rather sour, plainly not of the best. Then came the final prayer, and the people went out, neither depressed nor illumined with joy.... Only gradually, in the course of the following days, did it dawn on me that nothing had happened. I had reached the pinnacle of religious initiation, had expected something – I knew not what – to happen, and nothing at all had happened.... I came to understand that this communion had been a fatal experience for me. It had proved hollow; more than that, it had

> proved to be a total loss. I knew that I would never again be able to participate in this ceremony. "Why, that is not religion at all," I thought. "It is an absence of God; the church is a place I should not go to. It is not life which is there, but death."[10]

As one might imagine, being a pastor was no longer an option for Carl. Instead, he went into the psychiatric profession, there to eventually meet Freud, with whom he had a long, if conflicted, relationship. The tension manifested itself in terms of their divergent views on religion. Freud thought all religion was infantile, a cultural projection in disguised form of father conflicts. Jung, on the other hand, was destined to create a form of psycho-spirituality. A series of private, spiritual experiences proved crucial in his decision to embrace a spiritually charged form of psychology. He recounts sitting alone in his office, he began to sense the presence of spirit beings. These beings began to communicate with him, serving as his "ghostly gurus" as they shared higher spiritual wisdom. These spirit beings took control of him and, when he picked up a pen, dictated an entire book which "began to flow out of me, and in the course of three evenings the thing was written." This inward connection with a higher spiritual reality provided the nucleus of what was to become his psychological theory:

> Today I can say that I have never lost touch with my initial experiences. All my works, all my creative activity, has come from those initial fantasies and dreams.... Everything that I accomplished in later life was already contained in them, although at first only in the form of emotions and images.[11]

To find words and terminology with which he might create a new psycho-spirituality, Jung began scouring Asian religions and the texts of ancient mystics, adhering to what we might call the Western gnostic or esoteric traditions. Even to this day, many who begin reading Jungian psychology get their first introductions to these unconventional spiritual philosophies and take their first steps toward embracing the "combinativeness" we associate with being SBNR.

Among Jung's many theoretical contributions, a few are worthy of mention insofar as they are directly compatible with those who proclaim BSBNR. For example, the core of Jung's psycho-spirituality is the developmental backbone he called "individuation." The latter Jung defined as follows:

> Individuation means becoming an "in-dividual," and, in so far as "individuality" embraces our innermost, last, and incomparable uniqueness, it also implies becoming one's own self. We could therefore translate individuation as "coming to selfhood" or "self-realization."[12]

Jung believed that what he described "individuation" and "self-realization" are the aims of personal spiritual growth. He proclaimed that there is a deeper self within that guides the individual attuned to its messages. This guidance can be communicated through dreams, meaningful coincidences (which Jung termed "synchronicity"), intuition, neuroses and physical ailments of various kinds, and therapeutic intervention. Jung thought that all traditional religions could play a role in this. He made clear, however, that what is of value in religion was its unchurched, psychological, and experiential core. As he put it,

> I want to make clear that by "religion" I do not mean a creed.... Creeds are codified and dogmatized forms of original religious experience. The contents of the experience have become sanctified and usually congealed in a rigid, often elaborate, structure.[13]

Jung was giving voice to one of SBNR's core tenets. The goal of religion is not to induce consent to creeds but to facilitate direct encounters with a higher, divine reality. Fully individuating, fully realizing the totality of our potential selfhood requires a spiritual stance toward life. Insofar as traditional religion can offer images and experiences that foster connection with one's unconscious depths, so much the better. But Jung believed that a good many persons will remain stuck on the path to selfhood until they more fully explore alternative spiritual philosophies. Jungian Institutes and centers are religiously eclectic for this very reason. They understand themselves as resource centers for a pluralistic, eclectic approach to vital living.

To illustrate the influence of Jung on the SBNR mentality, we can fast forward to the present day and the way it helped the life of David, a 19-year-old undergraduate who was grieving the sudden death of Randy, a lifelong friend. Upon being admitted to college, David moved several hundred miles from his rural home, where Randy had died in his hometown. In relating stories about Randy, David explored his feelings of loss and guilt at having left his hometown. The turning point came when he had a dream, which he brought to his therapist. In that dream, Randy was still alive and they were talking and laughing together. As the dream ended, Randy handed David a quarter, which he took, puzzled. On waking, David found that he had a quarter in his hand, which he found to be both uncanny and troubling. David went to some pains to deny that it could have appeared in any conventional way (e.g., that change might have fallen out of his pocket on the bed before he fell asleep), a denial that reflected both the uncanny nature of the experience and the ways in which its uncanniness was essential to its meaning. Slowly, with the help of his therapist, he began to understand it as a communication from Randy. David was often short on funds, and Randy often helped him with the few extra coins he needed to buy a soda or a burger. Randy's generosity, then, was a critical part of their relationship. David came to understand the dream as reflecting their enduring connection and also as a charge to honor him through his own acts of generosity—to allow Randy to live through him. The key to all this was Jung's notion of synchronicity, understood as an inner state connected to an external state in an a-causal way and experienced as a "meaningful coincidence." That concept gave David a useful frame to understand his experience and assuage his anxiety. David understood it as a spiritual experience, one that allowed the acute symptoms of his grief to lift and directed him into a gently enhanced ethical relatedness. It was this "unchurched" psycho-spiritual framing of his grief and his dream, then, that allowed David to work through his grief, enabling a potentially crippling event to become integrated into his process of self-affirmation and individuation.

SUMMARY THOUGHTS

To summarize: we have characterized the beliefs/attitudes of those who are SBNR. We have also characterized the practices that are associated with being SBNR as well as some of the psychological traits associated with people who are drawn to this approach. In order to illustrate some of these elements in action, we have provided two case histories.

What is more difficult is deciding whether it is good or bad to be SBNR. How might someone who is wholly nonreligious critique those who are SBNR? How might someone who belongs to an established religious organization critique those who are SBNR? How valid are standard criticisms of being SBNR? The next chapter takes up these questions and helps us assess what be considered SBNR's strengths and weaknesses.

NOTES

1 Robert Wuthnow, *After Heaven: Spirituality in America Since the 1950s* (Berkeley, CA: University of California Press, 1998).
2 George Ripley, cited in the overview of Transcendentalism found in Winthrop Hudson, *Religion in America* (New York, NY: Charles Scribner's Sons, 1973).
3 Ralph Waldo Emerson, included in Catherine Albanese, ed., *The Spiritual Writings of the American Transcendentalists* (Macon, GA: Mercer University Press, 1988), p. 48.
4 William James, "Address of the President Before the Society for Psychical Research (1896)," in Frederick Burkhardt, ed., *The Works of William James,* 14 vols. (Cambridge, MA: Harvard University Press, 1986), 14:131.
5 William James, *A Pluralistic Universe* (New York, NY: E. P. Dutton, 1909/1971), p. 266.
6 Meredith McGuire, "Mapping Contemporary American Spirituality," *Christian Spirituality Bulletin*, 5 (Spring 1997): 3–8.
7 Pew Research Center, "America's Changing Religious Landscape," online report, May 12, 2015, 3. https://www.pewresearch.org/religion/2015/05/12/americas-changing-religious-landscape/
8 See Robert C. Fuller, "Minds of Their Own: Psychological Substrates of the Spiritual but Not Religious Sensibility," in William B. Parsons, ed., *Being Spiritual but Not Religious: Past, Present, Future(s)* (New York, NY: Routledge, 2018), pp. 89–109.
9 Carl Jung, *Memories, Dreams, Reflections* (New York, NY: Vintage, 1989), pp. 39–40.
10 Carl Jung, *Memories, Dreams, Reflections* (New York, NY: Vintage, 1989), pp. 54–55.

11 Carl Jung, *Memories, Dreams, Reflections* (New York, NY: Vintage, 1989), p. 199.
12 Carl Jung, *Two Essays on Analytical Psychology* (Princeton, NJ: Princeton University Press, 1966), p. 173.
13 Carl Jung, *Psychology and Religion* (New Haven, CT: Yale University Press, 1938), p. 6.

BIBLIOGRAPHY

Albanese, C. ed., *The Spiritual Writings of the American Transcendentalists*. Macon, GA: Mercer University Press, 1988.

Fuller, R.C. "Minds of Their Own: Psychological Substrates of the Spiritual but Not Religious Sensibility," in W.B. Parsons, ed., *Being Spiritual but Not Religious: Past, Present, Future(s)*. New York, NY: Routledge, 2018, pp. 89–109.

Homans, P. *Jung in Context*. Chicago, IL: The University of Chicago Press, 1979.

Hudson, W. *Religion in America*. New York, NY: Charles Scribner's Sons, 1973.

James, W. *A Pluralistic Universe*. New York, NY: E. P. Dutton, 1909/1971.

James, W. "Address of the President Before the Society for Psychical Research (1896)," in F. Burkhardt, ed., *The Works of William James*, 14 vols. Cambridge, MA: Harvard University Press, 1986.

Jung, C. *Psychology and Religion*. New Haven, CT: Yale University Press, 1938.

Jung, C. *Two Essays on Analytical Psychology*. Princeton, NJ: Princeton University Press, 1966.

Jung, C. *Memories, Dreams, Reflections*. New York, NY: Vintage, 1989.

McGuire, M. "Mapping Contemporary American Spirituality," *Christian Spirituality Bulletin*, 5 (Spring 1997): 3–8.

Pew Research Center, "America's Changing Religious Landscape," online report, May 12, 2015.

Wuthnow, R. *After Heaven: Spirituality in America Since the 1950s*. Berkeley, CA: University of California Press, 1998.

5

CRITICISMS AND DEBATES

Being spiritual but not religious (SBNR) has its critics. Members of traditional religious organizations are upset by how far it strays from traditional religious authority. They claim that those who are SBNR pick and choose only what appeals to them personally. To them, being SBNR is all about the human self rather than being all about God. This "excessive" individualism is a criticism shared even by many cultural observers who aren't all that religious. They, too, see SBNR as a prime example of how modern individuals have lost any sense of community or social responsibility. And, finally, those committed to a wholly secular or nonreligious outlook find SBNR lacking in intellectual merit. They see SBNR as embracing vague, fuzzy supernatural ideas that have no more intellectual merit than do traditional religions.

Like all debates about religion, the issues raised by these criticisms do not admit of easy resolution. This chapter will try to provide an even-handed overview of these critiques and, in the process, reveal additional perspectives on what it means to be SBNR.

TRADITIONAL RELIGION'S PROBLEMS WITH SBNR

Spokespersons for organized religion find SBNR disorganized and amateurish. Few SBNR authors or lecturers have anywhere near the formal theological education of their churched counterparts. Their writings consequently lack the polish and sophistication that are found in those of professional

DOI: 10.4324/9781003604259-5

theologians. SBNR writings are often inconsistent in what they say about how more-than-physical energies can affect events in the physical world (i.e., how spiritual forces might influence our health, our relationships, or our economic well-being). Most of these alternative philosophies aren't very systematic. They often come across as a patchwork of disconnected ideas. Whereas most religious writings utilize vocabulary created by centuries of shared theological tradition, unchurched traditions are more idiosyncratic and tend to imitate faddish trends in popular culture.

One of SBNR's core attitudes is believing that it is not just the right, but even the duty of everyone to decide what is true for themselves. This attitude is precisely what troubles those who are traditionally religious. Religion is about submitting to a higher authority. It is no coincidence that the world's second largest (and fastest growing) religion is Islam—a word that literally means "submission": submission to God; submission to the Qur'an; submission to male authorities. Judaism and Christianity are also religions that insist on submission and obedience: obedience to God; obedience to the Bible; and obedience to male religious officials. SBNR's individualism flies in the face of this deference to divine authority. It is for this very reason that a form of spirituality is charged with perpetuating rather than mitigating human sin.

Typical SBNRers don't hold a fixed set of beliefs. Their beliefs are loosely held and constantly changing. There are, however, many common themes in how SBNRers conceptualize God, human nature, and the afterlife. Virtually, all of these themes are considered heresy in the three main Bible-based religions (Judaism, Christianity, and Islam). This clash in theological outlooks is particularly evident in SBNR's almost total indifference to the concepts of sin. For Bible-based religions, sin means to disobey God. This includes disobeying rules laid down in the Bible (God's word) and laid down by ordained clergy (God's worldly representatives). Indeed, the central purpose of the three Bible-based religions is in some way helping humans repair the afterlife consequences of their sinful disobedience. SBNRers simply don't accept this fundamental notion of sin as disobedience. They agree with traditional religion that most humans are estranged from God (typically viewed by SBNRers as an immanent divine presence). But SBNRers believe that this estrangement stems from the fact that we have not yet sufficiently made an inward connection with this indwelling presence or power—not because of disobeying biblical commands. To be sure, some traditional western traditions would agree with this insofar as the estrangement is due to not accepting that we are already reconciled to God. For this reason, being SBNR doesn't require submitting to a bible, an ordained church official, or a religious institution. SBNers thus remain outside the control of religious authority. And, to someone committed to traditional modes of religiosity, this means that SBNR's "picking and choosing" approach to belief is destined to be a path leading away from eternal salvation.

The biblical religions have all come to terms with "evil" more fully than anything we find in the SBNR movement. Over long periods of time, religious communities must face tragedies of every kind: disease, horrible accidents, birth defects, poverty, violence, and mean or vicious behavior. Ordained clergy (ministers, priests, rabbis, imams) provide pastoral counseling and learn how religious faith might serve as a resource for coping with human tragedy. SBNR has far less to offer someone experiencing extreme loss or hardship. It has no articulated response to tragedy. Though traditional religion cannot prevent misfortune, it has surely proven more capable of sustaining humans through their most difficult times than the SBNR movement has yet demonstrated.

Those coming from a traditionally religious background find SBNR lacking even when it comes to inward-looking spirituality. They often note the superficial nature of the mystical spirituality these systems promote. Newcomers to the movement are encouraged to dabble in spiritual practices without the rigorous discipline associated with the mystical traditions of the world's major religions. Classical mystical texts depict a path requiring years of sustained asceticism, often including fasting or celibacy. Classical mysticism also includes disciplined prayer and exercise aimed at cultivating humility and the submission of one's personal will to the higher authority of God. SBNR systems are considerably less demanding.

Those attracted to these systems appear to seek out mystical experience to reassure themselves of the existence of any kind of more-than-physical reality. It seems, however, that they are usually content to "return" from their supernatural experiences and leave this higher reality at the far fringes of their daily lives. Put differently, encounters with a higher, metaphysical reality rarely upset individuals' previously defined lifestyle, interests, or values. Sociologist Robert Wuthnow suggests that these forms of mysticism are therefore shallow. He claims they rarely prompt people to rearrange their priorities. Paranormal events not only reinforce the belief that the supernatural exists but also persuade people that the supernatural cannot in any way be understood and, therefore, it need not take much of their time. The supernatural remains a mysterious force, not something that is revealed in an authoritative text or institution.[1]

And without such authoritative guidance, mystical quests lead modern seekers right back to the kinds of consumer lifestyles they enjoyed all along.

SBNR AND SPIRITUAL NARCISSISM

Many aligned with traditional religion fault SBNR because it doesn't require engagement with a community. A great deal of being SBNR is about individual belief and individual practice. There are many settings where like-minded spiritual seekers find camaraderie and companionship (meditation classes, seminars/lectures, weekend retreats, online communities, etc.), but it isn't required or structured in the way that it is for members of a synagogue or church. Religious institutions have served as a primary source of community over the course of Western history. They have—for better or for worse—helped socialize individuals into a shared communal outlook. Being SBNR doesn't generate the same kind of institutions capable of forging community bonds.

There are many cultural observers outside organized religion who also see the SBNR movement as yet another example of the erosion of communal bonds in modern life. As early as the 1980s, sociologist Robert Bellah and a group of scholars explored how the growing presence of individualism has affected American society. They interviewed a young nurse named Sheila Larson, who told them: "I believe in God. I'm not a religious fanatic. I can't remember the last time I went to church. My faith has carried me a long way. It's Sheilaism. Just my own little voice."[2] These scholars were quick to point out that "Sheilaism" was a symptom of how disconnected modern people are from their broader communities. Sheila didn't commit steadfastly to church teachings; she instead patched together her own set of religious beliefs guided only by her own inner voice. The danger of Sheilaism, according to these scholars, is that it fails to connect individuals with any particular community or to any particular religious practice. In the long run, Sheilaism deprives us of a language genuinely able to mediate among self, society, and the natural world. Such spiritual philosophies tend to fall back on abstractions when talking about the most important things. They stress "communication" as essential to relationships without adequately considering what is to be communicated. They talk about "relationships" but cannot point to the personal virtues and cultural norms that give relationships "meaning and value."[3]

The charge against being SBNR, then, is that it devolves into "spiritual narcissism." It does so by valorizing the individual. Most of those who embrace being SBNR reject traditional religious beliefs concerning humanity's innate sinfulness and even proclaim that that the divine is to be found within. This privatized form of religion ignores any notion that places the needs of the group above the needs of the individual. The danger is that the endless pursuit of self-realization steers us away from building a better world. In his best-selling book *The Road Less Travelled*, the psychiatrist M. Scott Peck summarizes this critique:

> Americans have retreated to purely personal preoccupations … people have convinced themselves that what matters is psychic self-improvement: getting in touch with their feelings, eating health food, taking lessons in ballet or belly-dancing, immersing themselves in the wisdom of the East, overcoming the "fear of pleasure", jogging, learning how to

> "relate." Harmless in themselves, these pursuits, elevated to a program and wrapped in the rhetoric of authenticity and awareness, signify a retreat from politics and a repudiation of the recent past.[4]

The kind of inwardness that the SBNR movement admires is both a symptom and a cause of Western culture's progressive loss of communal commitments. The most forceful exposition of this view was penned by Jeremy Carrette and Richard King in their co-authored book titled *Selling Spirituality*. They explicitly link being SBNR to neoliberal capitalism, pop media, and its consumer culture. To make their case, their genealogy of the historical trajectory of SBNR deviates only slightly from the one offered in our opening pages in order to emphasize the complicity of neoliberal capitalism. In their view, being SBNR came to be siphoned through two major historical movements: (1) the enlightenment stress on the privatization of religion and focus on the individual; and (2) the subsequent twentieth-century "corporatization of spirituality" in which neoliberalism has tailored individual desires for self-fulfillment for the purpose of reproducing the capitalistic ethos of growth, industrial efficiency, profitability, and success. Their critique, insofar as it focuses on neoliberal capitalism, highlights the economic and cultural analyses offered by Karl Marx and Michel Foucault. But their narrative also emphasizes how psychology plays a pivotal role in the formation of being SBNR and its myopic focus on the individual. In particular, it is William James, whose writings privatized and democratized religious experience, and then Abraham Maslow and his Humanistic psychology that are singled out.

With respect to Maslow, recall that his humanistic psychology emphasizes the theme of personal growth. In his view, the satisfaction of a person's basic physiological needs and those for safety, love, belonging, and self-esteem necessarily leads to the additional search for "peak experiences." In Carrette and King's view, this way of framing how happiness and meaning are achieved in a person's life is fed by a neoliberal culture, which values and supports the theme of ever-renewed "growth." They ask the question: what social conditions led to the formation of Maslow's psychology? Their answer is that the period right after Second World War, which saw the valorization of technology, an "executive" ego, and the steroidal development of a neoliberal, capitalistic economy and culture, became the soil that all but "invented" a psychology of growth and ever-renewed growth. Throw in the self-help pop culture, represented by luminaries such as Oprah and Deepak Chopra, and one has evidence of what Christopher Lasch, in his book *The Culture of Narcissism*, proclaims, namely, that social shifts have led to a form of spirituality beset by navel-gazing and narcissism.

A CONTRARY VIEW

Carrette and King's analysis has often been taken to be the defining scholarly lens through which the SBNR is understood. To be sure, they have a point. Other books in this genre have proliferated. For example, Kathryn Lofton's book on Oprah frames her as advocating a form of spiritual consumerism complete with an idealized spiritual figure (Oprah herself) who promotes books, practices, therapies, and a secular spiritual gospel designed to foster growth, renewal and self-transformation. Lofton sees Oprah as a uniquely American product in its appeal to individualism, wealth and, at times, narcissism, turning spirituality into a marketable product.[5] At the same time, we may ask whether there exist other forms of being SBNR that such studies fail to take into account. For example, a balanced view of the Transcendentalist philosopher Ralph Waldo Emerson shows him to be less a self-absorbed navel-gazer than a mature, reflective thinker helping Americans understand how they might avoid a life of mindless conformity to unexamined social norms. Meanwhile, fellow Transcendentalist Margaret Fuller was not only a respected journalist and editor but is often framed as one of the most powerful early proponents for women's rights. Howard Thurman was yet another writer with links to the SBNR movement who advocated a religious outlook, which featured commitments to social justice and inclusion. Thurman co-founded the Church for the Fellowship of all Peoples, which still exists in San Francisco and can be characterized as a social space for those professing being SBNR. Historian Leigh Schmidt's work *Restless Souls* is the scholarly proponent of this view in emphasizing how the liberal Protestant tradition was a facilitator for the thought and impact of individuals such as Emerson, Fuller, and Thurman, thus providing a corrective to the kinds of critiques offered by scholars like Carrette and King. As he puts it:

> ... if we really want to do something about narcissism and selfishness, about loose religious and civic connections, about the intolerant narrowness of fundamentalist orthodoxies, about the hubris of empire, we need to work with what got us here – a robust liberal tradition with strong religious elements.... The spirituality that those principles have produced revels in the religious experience of free and equal individuals, in the development of meditative interiority, in the cultivation of solitude and silence, in artful lives of creative self-expression. At the same time, it has also been committed to the search for community, the mutual understanding of differences, the constitution of meaningful identities, and the creation of unifying alliances across global divides.[6]

There are empirical studies that back Schmidt's view. In linked essays, Dillon et al (2003) and Wink et al (2005) gathered data on the SBNR movement, focusing on the relation between spirituality, narcissism, and psychotherapy (with a specific emphasis on Maslow and Humanistic forms of therapeutic intervention). They note that no empirical studies have yet attempted to empirically adjudicate between two reigning perspectives on the therapeutic, namely, what they refer to as the "cultural criticism" hypothesis (aligned with Carrette and King) and the "self-growth/self-realization" hypothesis (aligned with humanistic forms of psychotherapy). The latter states that successful therapeutic intervention leads to a more cohesive self, personal autonomy, and social generativity. These studies confirm, as with Carrette and King, that some of their findings support the "cultural criticism" perspective when it is linked to a depleted self and archaic or pathological narcissism. On the other hand, their findings, as with Schmidt, "do not support the general claim that an individuated spirituality is antithetical to communal commitment and they challenge any simple model that postulates an inevitable dichotomy between an institutionally autonomous spirituality and concern for others."[7] When faced with what they call "autonomous or healthy narcissism," which is the desired outcome of psychotherapeutic intervention, they conclude that the significance of their study lies in showing that such therapeutically transformed spirituality "is associated with a healthy form of narcissism characterized by personal autonomy with concern for the welfare of future generations."[8]

One may also add more empirical evidence, this time with respect to Carl Jung's psychology, which we have framed as a cultural contributor to being SBNR. His core concept of individuation is sometimes confused with narcissistic, solipsistic self-involvement. But individuation always occurs in a complex relationship to the communal whole. In fact, there are many writers and educators following in the Jungian tradition who have noted the communal and political implications of this core Jungian principle in ways that are increasingly connected to direct social action. For example, the Jungian analyst Andrew Samuels suggests that "experiences in therapy act to fine down generalized rage into a more specific format, hence rendering emotion more accessible for social action."[9] Again, the post-Jungian scholar and psychotherapist Stephen Aizenstat coined the term "archetypal activism" to express his vision of a social action that emerges from a psychospiritual interiority. He advocated for a therapeutic practice that emerges from attention to one's dream life in which specific actions inspired by the dreams would be "rooted in something deeper than political gain or enhanced self-esteem."[10] As founder of the Pacifica Graduate Institute, which provides accredited graduate academic and clinical training and is one of the leading post-Jungian intellectual hubs, Aizenstat's vision of social action grounded in therapeutic introspection and healing has had an increasing influence in Western society.

This characterization extends to the Jungian institutional structure. While the original Jungian institutions were focused on clinical training (and their social engagement typically took the form of low-fee psychotherapeutic clinics that serve the poor), an increasing number of contemporary Jungian organizations serve, and are sometimes led by, the (typically well-educated) general public. They are access points to a Jungian psycho-spirituality, serving as nodes around which new spiritual communities continue to emerge. While precisely how they engage the broader community varies from group to group, a good illustration can be found in the Jung Center of Houston. Founded in 1958 by five Houston women, only one of whom had any formal analytic training, the offerings of this center suggest a more complex and socially engaged profile that resists superficial critiques of therapeutic culture and contemporary spiritualities. Since 1997, the Center has provided psychoeducational classes for homeless and underserved children in partnership with neighborhood-based nonprofit organizations. The Center works to mitigate the effects of vicarious trauma with county forensic investigators, case managers for K-12 students in low-socioeconomic areas of the region, public health workers, frontline social service professionals working with children in both the child welfare and juvenile justice systems, and other similar populations. All of these offerings have been provided free of charge to the participants.

Jungian social service also has an international reach. A relevant, special case is recent work done in Haiti with the University of Notre Dame of Port au Prince and CESSA (the Center for Spirituality and Mental Health in Port au Prince). In helping to train paraprofessionals to work with traumatized Haitians, The Jung Center introduced trainees to a psychological understanding of spirituality drawn from William James and post-Jungian thought. Conference organizers suggested that this psychologized spirituality could prove an important tool in opening dialogue between the Christian social service providers and the local community of Vodou healers, a dialogue intended to advance mental health education nationwide.[11]

Finally, Theologian Linda Mercadante has interviewed and gathered extensive qualitative/quantitative information about those who profess to be SBNR. Interestingly, she finds that SBNRers hold diverse opinions toward institutional religion. While some are completely without any attachments to institutional religion, others have maintained a certain degree of affiliation. These latter individuals still find value in communal worship but do so in ways that integrate wide-ranging ideas and private practices. In other words, being SBNR often shades into being spiritual *and* religious.[12] Many of those who are spiritual *and* religious would value communal connections as much as individuals who are traditionally religious. The point here is that we need to be very clear about who we have in mind before we even begin to think about whether they might be characterized as "spiritual narcissists."

In sum, being SBNR is a multi-faceted phenomenon, which admits of a broad spectrum of psych-social types both historically and in the contemporary setting.

SECULAR CRITIQUES OF SBNR

Those who identify themselves as "wholly nonreligious" have their own critiques of being SBNR. These critiques are intellectual in nature. They have to do with judgments about what constitutes the most reliable form of thinking or reasoning. Nonreligious thinkers typically identify with the Western scientific tradition. What we commonly refer to as "the scientific method" can be traced back to the ancient Greek philosopher Aristotle who maintained that all knowledge must first come through the physical senses. Observation—not some intuitive feeling—is the cornerstone of sound reasoning. Over the centuries, scientists added such additional elements of sound observation-based reasoning (known as empiricism or the empirical method): a public openness about how the observations were obtained; forming hypotheses that might explain observations; and the necessity of verifying hypothesis through rigorous verification processes. This empirical method of knowing has given rise to almost everything we value in modern life: scientific medicine, electronics, computers, heating/refrigeration, transportation, etc. Empiricism and the evidence-based reasoning it supports have thus given rise to the major advances in human history. Most advocates of this scientifically grounded outlook on life have therefore become skeptical of the kinds of evidence-free "intuitions"—especially those fostering belief in the supernatural.

There are, of course, many versions of modern secular philosophy. But almost all are wary of the kind of SBNR's intuition-driven reasoning. It should be clear that secular critiques of spiritual thinking apply to traditional religion (e.g., belief in angels, belief in miracles, belief in unobserved things such as souls, heaven, hells, etc.) every bit as much as they apply to SBNR (e.g., belief in subtle spiritual energies, belief in auras, belief in any divine presence, etc.). Secular philosophy finds any and all spiritual thinking to be naïve and guilty of magical reasoning.

Secular philosophy finds that SBNR's magical thinking causes it to underestimate life's complexity. Spiritual thinking is based on an intuitive faith in the existence of higher powers that can somehow enter into and exert causal influence in our world. This intuitive faith leads us to focus on the beliefs and practices that can coax higher powers into working on our behalf. Prayer, meditation, reciting affirmations, and ritual practices all seek to open this world to the inflow of higher spiritual energies. Advocates of secular philosophies, however, find all of this to be literally nonsense. That is, these ideas are not supported by sensory-based or empirical reasoning. Spiritual beliefs are nonsense ideas. And, as such, they lack the intellectual merit that we find in science-based ideas. Spiritual thinking simply ignores both common sense and all that we scientifically know about the world. It lacks connection with our accumulated knowledge about the biological, psychological, economic, and social factors that actually do influence events in our world. Spiritual thinking therefore perpetuates our brain's inherent tendencies toward magical thinking. For this reason, it often stands in the way of making slow but steady progress in solving life's problems. Spirituality's magical qualities prevent people from adopting what might be called a "moral realism" that (1) acknowledges the complex factors impeding human progress and (2) calculates systematic strategies that skillfully address these factors.

The bottom line: secular philosophies deem any and all forms of spiritual thinking to be naïve and ineffective. They argue that if we want to improve our lives, we must first abandon the delusional fantasies of spiritual intuition in favor of a this-worldly philosophy.

ASSESSING THE CRITIQUES

All of these criticisms have at least some merit. The important question, however, is how we should judge or evaluate these criticisms. Each of the criticisms is based on a particular set of premises about what we think is the "proper" role of either religion or reason in our lives. Whether we agree or disagree with these criticisms thus has a lot to do with how fully we accept their premises. Each of us needs to ask whether we are already committed to a traditionally religious viewpoint. Are we already committed to a wholly secular outlook? Or do we find ourselves in some kind of third category, a category that falls under the umbrella of being SBNR? Our final judgment about the pros and cons of being SBNR (or being either traditionally religious or wholly nonreligious) is determined by where we are each coming from. This chapter can't resolve the age-old debates surrounding religion. But we can examine these critiques and consider their relative strengths and weaknesses.

The purely secular criticisms of SBNR are probably the fairest. Those who are committed to a purely rational or empirical approach to life typically oppose all religious thinking. They are typically even-handed in calling out both churched and unchurched forms of spiritual thinking. Criticizing SBNR for its frequent evocation of magical/supernatural thinking deserves a fair hearing.

The critiques of SBNR leveled by those committed to traditional religious organizations are not as even-handed. We might, for example, examine the charge that our unchurched spiritualities foster narcissism. This is an especially curious accusation given the fact that ardent Christians boldly proclaim that "Jesus loves me" and that God watches over them. Most people convert to Christianity in the hope of procuring individual salvation. And, too, most traditionally religious people believe in the power of prayer to coax God into acting on their behalf. The most common form of prayer is petitionary prayer—praying so that we or those we love get special treatment. It is true that SBNR individuals are more narcissistic than wholly nonreligious people. But so, too, are traditionally religious people.[13] In fact, the two categories of spiritually oriented people are basically equal when it comes to being narcissistic, so perhaps the question should be narcissistic compared to whom?

We might also ask what various critics mean by the term "narcissism." It has different meanings depending on whether it is invoked in everyday conversation, measured by the social scientific metric called the Narcissistic Personality Inventory, or used by psychotherapists trained in psychoanalysis. In everyday language, the word means "excessive interest in the self." The NPI scale used by social psychologists offers quantitative measurements of different facets related to excessive self-interest.

As noted in a previous section, the view of narcissism held by psychotherapists who are informed by the object relations and self-theory schools of psychoanalytic thought might shed some additional light on this issue. They distinguish between "healthy narcissism" and "unhealthy narcissism." They have a great deal of clinical evidence to suggest that full psychological health requires a healthy self-love (a strong self-concept). What they call "healthy narcissism" requires individuals to believe that they are loved and prized by a "higher Other." This higher other might be an idealized parent or romantic partner. Or it might be an idealized more-than-physical "other" with whom we in some way merge or connect. The alternative spiritualities we have covered understand this very well. They offer both beliefs and practices that enable individuals to feel connected with, and empowered by, such a "higher Other." Being SBNR is very much about experiencing inward harmony with a divine presence. And, in the process, it promotes optimal psychological health. Healthy narcissism provides the inner security required by individuals to reach out to the surrounding world in confident and creative ways. It also protects them from the "unhealthy narcissism," which stems from too little—not too much—self-love. Individuals bereft of genuine self-love are fated to a life motivated by a deep-seated craving for praise and affirmation. For this reason, they display the manipulativeness and outward vanity we typically associate with being narcissistic. SBNR beliefs and practices might be as successful in eliciting healthy narcissism as anything available in contemporary culture. Traditional religions often provide similar beliefs and practices for feeling oneself prized and loved by a divine "other." But for many people, the God of traditional religion is remote, harsh, and inaccessible.

The phenomenon of Sheilaism may be discomforting to church officials whose professional identity is threatened when people openly pick and choose. But we need to consider the possibility that Sheila demonstrated a high level of religious maturity. She managed to find—and listen to—her own voice. This young woman gradually accepted responsibility for owning her own system of beliefs. She was able to differentiate between various religious concepts and identify which were most closely connected with her life. She developed a sense of personal relationship to God and translated the love and power she gained from this relationship into concrete acts of caring for others. Sheila learned to listen to her own inner voice and to be her own authority. The fact that so many of our contemporaries are taking paths similar to Sheila's could be taken as a sign of maturity and authenticity, even if it does result in fewer traditional believers.

Robert Bellah and his colleagues were probably right that Sheilaism is often associated with difficulty in identifying a coherent cultural vision. They argued that many who become SBNR stress the importance of communication without adequately considering what is worth communicating. They also argued that SBNRers stress relationships without adequately considering what virtues and moral principles give relationships meaning. This objection has some merit. But, again, compared to whom? Fair play requires us to apply evaluative criteria evenly. How many of those who belong to a Protestant Catholic, Jewish, or Muslim congregation have anything profound to offer on these topics? In fact, we might argue that our unchurched spiritualities approach these topics with more exploration and reflection than their churched counterparts. Contemporary seekers are typically aware of the moral challenges that arise in modern life. But they are skeptical of easy answers. And they are especially skeptical of "answers" based on texts or teachings that originated in ancient times. All SBNRers may not have a polished cultural vision. But they have identified some of the perspectives that they believe any such vision must include. They have affirmed the relevance of scientific, racial, gender, and ecological points of view and are unwilling to settle for cultural visions that omit them.

Similar considerations arise when considering the common charge that SBNR does little to form communities. We might, again, ask compared to whom? The fact that traditionally religious individuals file in and out of worship services each week doesn't in itself indicate participation in any community. We might also ask whether it is appropriate to link spirituality with community building per se. After all, every major religious tradition is full of stories about ancient mystics seeking visions of the divine in total solitude. And, interestingly, both art and music offer sublime experiences. But how often do we insist that our artistic or musical interests must necessarily be done in a public, organized fashion? Need one join a "Mozart Fan Club" or a "Picasso Fan Club" and march inside a special building once a week to attend a prearranged service dedicated to this—and only this—one musician or artist? So why is it different when it comes to our desire for some form of spirituality? Why insinuate that spiritual interests—to be genuine—must lead to institutional membership?

It is important to note that unchurched seekers actually do engage social spaces and institutions where SBNR ideas are exchanged. For example, one could point to retreat centers such as the Esalen Institute and events such as Burning Man that promote an eclectic orientation to traditional religions. Similarly, Jung Centers offer an array of practices and teachings taken from a variety of religious traditions.

Unitarian-Universalist churches across the country are also settings where seekers gather and share their spiritual journeys. Bohemian coffee shops have served as conversational settings for all things metaphysical since the rise of the Beatnick and hippie movements in San Francisco and New York's Greenwich Village. The same can be said of bookstores featuring large sections labeled "Eastern Religions," "New Age," and "The Occult." Unchurched spirituality is disseminated in decentralized ways without the benefit of core doctrines and rituals that are repeated at the exact same time and place each week. But they are nonetheless often disseminated through face-to-face human interactions.

The charge that many unchurched seekers explore spiritual systems in a superficial way is probably true. We might, however, note that a full 9% of the American population can be classified as "highly active seekers," meaning that they are deeply invested in their ongoing journeys.[14] But undoubtedly, the majority of those who tell pollsters they identify as SBNR are less committed to specifically spiritual matters. The same is also true of those who belong to traditional religious institutions. Attendance can be sporadic. Attendance can also be superficial, with no intention of really changing one's overall values or time commitments because of anything said in a sermon or homily. Many Catholics today identify themselves as "cafeteria Catholics," openly admitting that they pick and choose from church teachings as they see fit. Are they more superficial than "loyal" Catholics who never pause and question anything? The question, again, is superficial compared to whom?

A related criticism of being SBNR is that the quest for mystical or paranormal events doesn't seem to alter their everyday commitments or priorities. Most seem totally comfortable in their lives as middle-class citizens in a capitalistic society. And once again, compared to whom? Protestant evangelicals are fully at home with middle-class culture and even boast that "being saved" is a sure ticket to social, economic, and even athletic prosperity. Those who pursue their spiritual journeys outside established churches are probably not much better on this score. This should not, however, prevent us from acknowledging that their fascination with supernatural phenomena performs a vital function in their lives. Those attracted to metaphysical topics and mystical experiences are not deciding between biblical religion and SBNR. They are instead debating whether, in good personal conscience, they can claim to believe in any kind of religion or spirituality at all. Most realize that secular understandings of the world have considerable intellectual authority. The role that science and technology play in our lives is proof positive of the value of adopting an outlook that casts doubt on anything that even hints of the supernatural. Today's unchurched seekers know that if they are to embrace any kind of spiritual outlook, they must do so in a way that doesn't try to defend ancient bibles over and against modern science. They require some kind of evidence indicating that our universe cannot be exhaustively explained by science. They, like William James before them, are in search of white crows. They are seeking a single event that proves that—at least occasionally—our world receives an influx from a spiritual "more." The SBNR movement is an expression of this modern spiritual hunger. SBR testimonies concerning mystical or paranormal experiences help prevent many from forever shutting the door to religion altogether. A sound argument can be made that anything that helps hold this door open is of spiritual value, even if many people understandably play it safe and linger near the entranceway.

We might, finally, consider the accusation that unchurched traditions tend to minimize the presence of tragedy in our lives. This comes with the further accusation that they underestimate the complex factors that cause—or alleviate—such tragedy. These critiques identify the fact that SBNR philosophies teach that we have the resources within ourselves to overcome the challenges confronting us in life. A common belief among SBNRers is that we have the power to create our own reality. In some instances, this devolves into sheer delusional thinking. Beginning with the New Thought movement in the late 1800s, some have argued that thoughts are themselves the most potent forces in the universe. Many teach that thoughts are capable of invisibly going out into the material universe and magically altering reality in conformity with our personal desires. Similar claims are made about the "subtle energies" ostensibly activated in today's many meditation- and body-based spiritual systems. Unfortunately, experience shows us that thoughts do not wield causal power in the biological, chemical, economic, or political worlds. Thoughts themselves cannot cure cancer, stop global warming, end recessions leading to widespread unemployment, or curtail international conflicts. SBNR's penchant for preaching "the power of positive thinking" reveals the problems inherent in constructing a worldview centered solely on the individual perspective.

The individual perspective might, however, be a viable starting place for a viable spiritual outlook. It draws attention to one of our most important freedoms. We do not always have the freedom to control outer circumstances (disease, climate, economic reversals, international conflict). But we do always have the freedom to construct our attitude toward these circumstances. SBNR traditions show us how we might construct spiritual philosophies capable of engendering world-building strategies. They alert us to the ways that we are ourselves expressions of the ongoing creation of the universe. They urge us to see ourselves as part and parcel of the divine spirit that ultimately lies behind this evolving universe. In this sense, we are all agents of divine activity and can steer the world toward greater levels of wholeness and love. SBNR's confidence in the individual's power to achieve wholeness on the personal level is—at least potentially—a viable starting point for an outlook determined to achieve wholeness on all other levels of our interconnected worlds.

NOTES

1 Robert Wuthnow, *After Heaven: Spirituality in America Since the 1950s* (Berkeley, CA: University of California Press, 1998), p. 134.
2 Robert Bellah, Richard Madsen, William Sullivan, Ann Swidler, and Steven Tipton, *Habits of the Heart* (Berkeley, CA: University of California Press, 1985), p. 221.
3 Robert Bellah, Richard Madsen, William Sullivan, Ann Swidler, and Steven Tipton, *Habits of the Heart* (Berkeley, CA: University of California Press, 1985), p. 237.
4 See Jeremy Carrette and Richard King, *Selling Spirituality* (New York, NY: Routledge, 2005), p. 55.

5 Kathryn Lofton, *Oprah: The Gospel of an Icon* (Berkeley, CA: University of California Press, 2011).
6 Leigh Schmidt, *Restless Souls: The Making of American Spirituality* (San Francisco, CA: Harper, 2005), pp. 289–290.
7 Michelle Dillon, Paul Wink, and Kristen Fay, "Is Spirituality Detrimental to Generativity?" *Journal for the Scientific Study of Religion*, 42, no. 3 (2003): 438.
8 Wink, Paul, Michelle Dillon, and Kristen Fay, "Spiritual Seeking, Narcissism, and Psychotherapy: How Are They Related?" *Journal for the Scientific Study of Religion*, 44, no. 2 (2005): 156.
9 Andrew Samuels, *The Political Psyche* (London: Routledge, 1993), p. 51.
10 Stephen Aizenstat, *Dreamtending: Attending to the Healing Power of Dreams* (New Orleans, LA: Spring Journal Books, 2011), p. 171.
11 W. Jean-Charles, personal communication.
12 See Linda Mercadante, *Belief without Borders: Inside the Minds of the Spiritual but Not Religious* (New York, NY: Oxford University Press, 2014).
13 See Robert Fuller, "Minds of Their Own," in W.B. Parsons, ed., *Being Spiritual but Not Religious: Past, Present, Future(s)* (New York, NY: Routledge, 2018). See also Robert Fuller and Anthony Hermann, "Grandiose Narcissism and Religiosity," in Anthony Hermann, ed., *Handbook of Trait Narcissism* (New York, NY: Springer, 2018).
14 Wade Clark Roof, *A Generation of Seekers: The Spiritual Journeys of the Baby-Boom Generation* (San Francisco, CA: Harper, 1993), pp. 79–83.

BIBLIOGRAPHY

Aizenstat, S. *Dreamtending: Attending to the Healing Power of Dreams*. New Orleans, LA: Spring Journal Books, 2011.

Carrette, J. and R. King. *Selling Spirituality*. New York, NY: Routledge, 2005.

Dillon, M., P. Wink, and K. Fay. "Is Spirituality Detrimental to Generativity?" *Journal for the Scientific Study of Religion*, 42, no. 3 (2003): 427–442.

Freud, S. *The Psychopathology of Everyday Life*. New York, NY: Norton, 1965.

Fuller, R. *Spiritual, But Not Religious: Understanding Unchurched America*. New York, NY: Oxford University Press, 2001.

Homans, P. *Jung in Context*. Chicago, IL: The University of Chicago Press, 1975.

Homans, P. *The Ability to Mourn*. Chicago, IL: The University of Chicago Press, 1989.

James, W. *The Varieties of Religious Experience*. New York, NY: Modern Library, 1929.

Jung, C. *Psychology and Religion*. New Haven, CT: Yale University Press, 1938.
Jung, C. "Adaptation, Individuation, Collectivity," in *The Symbolic Life: Collected Works of C.G. Jung*, 18 vols, translated by R.F.C. Hull. Princeton, NJ: Princeton University Press, 1950, 18:449–454.
Kohut, H. "Forms and Transformations of Narcissism," in P. Ornstein, ed., *The Search for the Self*. New York, NY: International Universities Press, 1978, pp. 427–460.
Kohut, H. "On Leadership," in C. Strozier, ed., In *Self Psychology and the Humanities*. New York, NY: W.W. Norton, 1985, pp. 51–72.
Mercadante, L. *Belief without Borders: Inside the Minds of the Spiritual but Not Religious*. New York, NY: Oxford University Press, 2014.
Parsons, W.B. *The Enigma of the Oceanic Feeling*. New York, NY: Oxford University Press, 1999.
Parsons, W.B. ed. *Being Spiritual but Not Religious: Past, Present, Future(s)*. New York, NY: Routledge, 2018.
Parsons, W.B., D. Jonte-Pace, and S. Henking, eds. *Mourning Religion*. Charlottesville, VA and London: University of Virginia Press, 2008.
Rieff, P. *The Triumph of the Therapeutic*. New York, NY: Harper, 1966.
Samuels, A. *The Political Psyche*. London: Routledge, 1993.
Schmidt, L.E. *Restless Souls: The Making of American Spirituality*. San Francisco, CA: Harper, 2005.
Wink, P., M. Dillon, and K. Fay. "Spiritual Seeking, Narcissism, and Psychotherapy: How Are They Related?" *Journal for the Scientific Study of Religion*, 44, no. 2 (2005): 143–158.

6

GLIMPSING THE FUTURE

Public opinion polls now ask respondents to identify themselves by selecting just one of three principal religious categories: traditionally religious, wholly nonreligious, or spiritual but not religious (SBNR). Being SBNR, then, has thus become an established feature of Western societies. It is widely recognized as having an identifiable place right alongside our established religious institutions. Polls indicate that the SBNR movement has continued to grow over the past few decades. From about 19% in the 1990s, it now accounts for between 22% and 27% of the North American population. And we know that this number is highest among those under 40 years old—suggesting that this percentage will continue to climb.

Will this trend continue? Is it likely that SBNR's market share will steadily grow? Or has the trend already peaked? How much of it amounts to little more than a cultural fad that is likely to recede? What is the future of SBNR?

Predicting the future is virtually impossible. This is especially true when it comes to religion. We might, however, risk taking a quick glimpse forward. What trends are we likely to see in the near future? Glimpsing forward will require that we also keep an eye on SBNR's two "competitors." After all, being SBNR means affirming spiritual or supernatural belief just as do those who are traditionally religious. And being SBNR also means distancing oneself from our formal religious organizations (including their scriptures, doctrines, rituals, and authorities) just as do those who are wholly nonreligious.

DOI: 10.4324/9781003604259-6

Asking about the future of SBNR includes asking about the future of these other two religious options.

BEING "NOT RELIGIOUS" GOING FORWARD

Being "wholly nonreligious" is by far the smallest of the three main categories of contemporary American religiosity (but not so small in many Western European nations). It always has been. And, in all probability, it always will be.

We have two different terms for describing unbelief. The first is being an atheist. A theist is someone who believes in a human-like god (*theus*, in Greek). By putting the "a" in front, we signify being against belief in a human-like god. Atheists thus deny the existence of a Supreme Being. Some studies show that upwards of 40% of the populations of Sweden, Denmark, and Norway identify as atheist. The percentage is nearly as high in France. Polls have shown that about 19% of Canadians identify as atheist. In the United States, however, the percentage is much lower, perhaps only 2.4%. A second term for unbelief is being an agnostic. The Greek word *gnostic* means possessing secretive knowledge. By putting the "a" in front, we signify being against the view that anyone possesses valid religious or mystical knowledge. Agnostics thus assert that the human mind just isn't capable of knowing whether a supreme being does or doesn't exist. Agnostics claim we simply can't know one way or the other. In the United States, only about 4% identify as agnostics, but this number is at least 20% in many western European nations. We might note that the percentage of atheists and agnostics is much higher among those with very high levels of education. Scientists are in particular inclined to doubt the existence of a heavenly Supreme Being.

Back in the 1960s, most social scientists predicted what they called the progressive secularization of Western culture. They argued that advanced technological cultures will gradually abandon religious belief in favor of analytic reasoning and science. The secularization theory has some merit. It correctly understands that we are all the products of social conditioning. Social conditioning has changed dramatically in the modern world—at the expense of organized religion. No one religious group enjoys a monopoly, allowing it to control how we think or behave. As a consequence, few of us are pressured into conforming to a narrow worldview. Modern individuals learn about science. We learn about how people who live in other countries think and behave, teaching us how religions are the product of cultural conditioning. We have religious options unavailable to previous human generations. There are fewer social constraints that might prevent us from doubting older belief systems or from experimenting with newly discovered belief systems. Individuals are increasingly able to escape the social stigma that used to be attached to labels such as atheist or agnostic.

It is reasonable to think that these secularizing trend patterns will continue into the foreseeable future. We might therefore expect the number of people who identify as either atheists or agnostics to continue to climb. But for reasons that will be explained in the next section, there is probably a fixed limit on the number of people in any human society who will openly reject any or all religious beliefs. We are probably close to that limit now.

BEING "TRADITIONALLY RELIGIOUS" GOING FORWARD

There is one major problem with this theory about the gradual secularization of Western culture. It doesn't take into consideration the more universal traits that characterize the human species. Many of these are biologically grounded and hence highly resistant to social and cultural trends. Others are products of the human situation: we are finite and hence vulnerable in an ever-threatening universe.

The biological sources of human religiosity express themselves in and through the brain's more intuitive functions. Human brains were shaped by natural selection to solve the kinds of survival problems faced by our ancient ancestors. Many of our innate cognitive abilities make religious belief all but inevitable. Take, for example, humanity's need to detect causal agents (e.g., wolves or human enemies) operating in our vicinity. Any unexpected event—a sound, smell, or sight—triggers the brain to identify its source. This source might very well pose a great opportunity (our next meal) or a great threat (our death). Human brains thus evolved in ways that spontaneously and automatically guide us to detect the responsible causal agent. This is particularly the case when the cause of unexpected events is in some way ambiguous or not readily apparent. Human brains understandably attribute human-like desires, feelings, and intentions to the "causal agents" that surround us. In other words, we intuitively think that we are surrounded by unseen causal agents who have human-like traits. We intuitively believe in gods or spirit beings.

Our biological brains have also been genetically shaped to perform other cognitive tasks associated with religion. They dispose us toward dualistic thinking. That is, they predispose us to think that the world consists of both observable matter and something unobservable (mind, spirit). We thus naturally and intuitively embrace religious beliefs about the existence of souls or spirits despite the fact that we have never detected them with our physical senses. Our brains are similarly designed to "see" meaning or purpose in events even when no such meaning or purpose exists. For this reason, we readily see "God's design" or "divine messages" in otherwise random events. And, too, we are wired to experience emotions such as shame and guilt that can be manipulated in ways that lead us to seek forgiveness through submission to religious authority.

The point here is that as long as each new human generation inherits a biological brain, humans will be inclined toward supernatural or religious thinking. No kind of cultural or historical change alters human DNA. Human brains are simply disposed to embrace supernatural conceptions. Overriding this tendency takes training and deliberate effort. And thus it should come as no surprise that even most of those people who tell pollsters they lean toward agnosticism or atheism nonetheless also report intellectual interest in magical or supernatural topics (e.g., telepathy, reincarnation, ghosts, etc.).

Human beings have other traits that predispose them to religion that are not so much biological as they are inescapable characteristics of finite existence. The psychologist Sigmund Freud understood that the human species is everywhere confronted with two stark realities that trigger religious impulses: (1) life is difficult and fraught with danger and (2) we are a social species and must solve the problem of living together despite our many antisocial tendencies. The human condition is one of insecurity. We are powerless in the face of natural disasters, including fires, tornados, hurricanes, earthquakes, and floods. Our bodies fail us. They are prone to terminal illnesses, advanced age, and death. It only stands to reason that we seek out the protective strength of spirit beings. We try to procure their assistance using the same techniques we use to coax fellow human beings: flattery, promise-making, gift-giving, and downright begging. As Freud so forcefully argued, as long as humans face threats to their well-being, we will turn in desperation to parent-like spirits in search of their protection and comfort.

There is a second feature of the human condition responsible for the ubiquity of religion. We are a social species. We must cooperate. The behavior of other social species (e.g., ants or bees) is wholly under the control of instincts. Genetics alone ensures prosocial behavior. Humans, however, have vastly more complex brains. We are not governed by genetics alone. We have to rely on various cultural mechanisms to lessen our inherent selfishness. We can, for example, try to monitor each other's behavior and provide elaborate systems of reward or punishment. Yet we can't put a police officer at every doorstep. We can't have judges in every neighborhood. As Freud pointed out, this is why every human society invents beliefs about heavenly beings who monitor our behavior. These supernatural beings know all and see all. They reward all good behavior and punish every misdeed; if not in this life, then surely in the afterlife. The promise of heavenly paradise and the threat of eternal damnation induce at least some level of social cooperation. The famed evolutionary biologist E.O. Wilson put this a bit differently. Wilson recognized that social species such as ours cannot survive without mechanisms that steer individuals toward serving the good of the group. He saw how religion is among the most effective mechanisms that humanity has yet created to perform this vital task. Religion, he observed, "is above all the process by which individuals are persuaded to subordinate their immediate self-interests to the interests of the group."[1] Religion provides people with a tribal identity. It promises eternal rewards for all who conform to the group's moral code. As long as humans seek security in group membership, they will eagerly embrace a religious faith.

Humans feel most secure when they are members of a tightly knit society. We are tribal beings. We know that there is strength in numbers. We feel loyalty to our clan, tribe, nation, or faith. Pledging religious faith continues to be a crucial way of displaying our willful submission to the group's moral codes. As worldwide migration patterns accelerate, there will likely be corresponding pressure to reaffirm our tribal loyalties. This will, in all likelihood, lead to increasing public affirmations of those religious beliefs that demarcate one's own cultural tribe. We already see this to some extent both in Western Europe and North America. Increased concern over "cultural outsiders" leads to increased efforts to advertise and monitor allegiance to traditional religious identities. Religion thus appears likely to endure, and even prosper, in the future.

We might, finally, point out that all human beings wake up in the morning to find themselves alive in a universe they did not create. Finite creatures did not produce existence. We behold the universe in awe and wonder, curious about its Ultimate Cause. The human brain asks questions of meaning and purpose. We yearn to understand our individual lives, to see how we fit into the grander scheme. Many—probably most—of us have spiritual feelings. We wish to discover—and harmoniously adjust ourselves to—the unseen order of existence.

For all of these reasons, religion is not going to diminish in our lifetime. We have already identified two important conditions under which we might expect religiosity to morph into some version of SBNR: the absence of strong socialization powers through which cultures can effectively channel individuals into a single outlook and relative freedom from existential stress. In the next section, we will examine the probable future(s) of SBNR in settings characterized by these two conditions. It is important, however, that we note that the world will witness unprecedented population growth over the next century. This growth will largely occur in the poorest regions across the globe. It will be highly conservative forms of traditional religion—not any version of SBNR—that will predominate in the world's densely populated regions. These forms of traditional religion are most likely to be highly tribal in nature, binding individuals into cultural groups eager to promote their own well-being even when at the expense of other tribes.

Traditional religious institutions will retain their current cultural status in economically advanced Western nations. This is in part owing to the fact that life in these nations is likely to become more stressful. Levels of professed belief will undoubtedly rise above their current levels. Religious belief is, after all, a way of signaling commitment to one's socio-political identity. It is also a way of signaling alignment with existing authority (either authority within the religious community or within the socio-political realm, depending on which community appears vulnerable).

The probable increase in people openly professing belief will probably not lead to increased attendance at weekly services. Our established religious institutions will have strong and loyal memberships. But most believers will probably remain casual attendees. Claiming religious faith will mostly signal allegiance to particular ethnic identities. But it will rarely inform or change people's pre-existing set of interests and values (especially their political or economic values).

One final trend we are likely to observe among those who claim traditional religiosity: the kind of "combinativeness" we associate with SBNR will also characterize the wider array of supernatural interests found among those who profess affiliation with a religious heritage. Even though people might publicly claim loyalty to a religious tradition, they are likely to assimilate many of the supernatural or metaphysical ideas circulating in popular culture without realizing that these views are in any way incompatible. Humans are drawn to what is intuitive and spontaneous, and are thus unlikely to be restrained by strict theological principles. According to the individualization theory, traditional and institutionalized forms of religiosity will be increasingly replaced by more subjective ones detached from the church, individually chosen, and syncretistic in character.

BEING SBNR GOING FORWARD

Being SBNR will be a viable "third category" in North America and Western Europe for decades to come. We know that almost everyone has some level of supernatural belief and some desire to connect with an "unseen order." Our media-driven world will provide endless opportunities to learn about attractive spiritual ideas and practices. It is tempting to predict that SBNR will continue its recent decades of growth. It may soon become the norm in Western nations.

SBNR's growth will be limited, however, by the existential stress we are beginning to witness even in countries with advanced economies. Immigration patterns have heightened ethnic tensions and fueled the resurgence of tribal behaviors that demarcate the "insiders" from the "outsiders." Any and all economic uncertainties further heighten individuals' need to align themselves with traditional authority. The future of SBNR, then, is in some ways tied to Western culture's socio-economic-political future. Will this be a future that nourishes support of individualism and tolerance, or a future that fuels ethnic tensions and religious tribalism?

We might, too, remind ourselves that being SBNR means different things to different people. Only a few of those who identify as being SBNR are highly active seekers. Most people are too preoccupied with their daily activities to be very concerned about some "unseen order." And spiritual interests come and go at different points in our life journey. Being SBNR—much like being conventionally religious—ebbs and flows throughout our lives. Thus, even though about 30% of the population in Western nations might identify as SBNR, only between 5% and 10% will be highly active in their spiritual quests.

The most enduring feature of SBNR will be its "combinativeness." Scholars have traditionally used the word "syncretism" to refer to the way that people have blended different religious practices together despite the fact that they come from quite different theological traditions. Take, for example, the history of the world's largest religion—Christianity. Christian proclamations about Jesus as the risen Christ represent a creative blending of Jewish, Greek, and myriad pagan stories about dying-and-resurrecting gods. Almost all Christians take their major holidays of Christmas and Easter as part of a seamless faith. But Christmas as we know it today is actually a hybrid of Roman solstice festivals combined with Germanic winter feasts. What are commercially familiar as the Easter bunny and Easter egg hunts are similarly vaguely Christianized expressions of pagan spring fertility rites. Religious traditions absorb from their surroundings. Every major religious tradition in the modern world is the result of centuries of syncretism. But historically, this process is slow. Syncretism is rarely a self-conscious process. It occurs from the bottom up. Ideas or practices combine with little or no conscious deliberation. Officials of religious institutions initially resist contaminating their traditional faith by absorbing these foreign elements, yielding only when their popularity makes them impossible to expel.

Historian Catherine Albanese proposed using the word "combinativeness" to refer to the way that today's spiritual seekers connect metaphysical beliefs.[2] Unchurched combinativeness differs from traditional religious syncretism in a few ways. It is more deliberate. Individuals self-consciously adopt ideas or practices from sources they know are theologically diverse. They choose, experiment, and evaluate these concepts without any concern about whether they are theologically consistent with ancient scriptures. They also discard concepts and move on to new ones far more quickly. Unchurched combinativeness is thus more rapid than traditional religious syncretism, which usually transpires over centuries. And whereas syncretism typically entails beliefs or practices that connect families or communities, combinativeness is more individualistic and hence idiosyncratic.

Being SBNR is about choosing for oneself. It is therefore easily influenced by cultural trends. To some extent, this is a positive attribute. It displays interest in being relevant. This "trendiness" engages seekers and gives being SBNR a sense of discovery and excitement. It is thus in some ways a positive quality, especially when contrasted with unreflective adherence to the ideas and practices of ancient societies. SBNR's ever-shifting interests often, however, give it an aura of superficiality. It often seems as though SBNR is prone to rapidly changing phases. Books on metaphysical topics appear and vanish in merry-go-round fashion: guardian angels, near-death experiences, trance channeling, mindfulness meditation, crystal healing, Eastern mysticisms, secret body energies, the wisdom of ancient civilizations, etc. The criticisms that SBNR is prone to fads are, to this extent, justified. But these criticisms miss the central point: being SBNR entails seeking out an "unseen order" to the universe. The various "faddish topics" that circulate through SBNR all have this in common: they stimulate our metaphysical curiosity. For those to whom traditional religion is no longer a viable option, SBNR's fresh approach to the supernatural sustains their belief in the existence of an unseen order of existence.

FINAL THOUGHTS

All evidence suggests that being SBNR has become a permanent feature of Western society. It represents individuals from across demographic categories. In many Western countries, it comprises the largest segment of the religious population. It is thus now fully settled into the overall cultural landscape.

SBNR's increasing visibility needs to be matched by an increasing viability. That is, being SBNR must be sustainable. A sustainable spirituality is not just a transitional phase in someone's spiritual journey; it is the journey itself. It must be sustainable over an individual's entire life span. It must be sustainable for the wider society.

We noted in Chapter 1 that "being spiritual" has always been in some way connected with mysticism. It has always meant making an inward connection with the sacred. It requires becoming receptive to the inflow of spiritual forces or energies. In this sense, being spiritual is first and foremost about being inwardly receptive.

To be spiritual, then, is to become receptive to an unseen order of life. Those who consider themselves SBNR think of this unseen order as a sacred order. They think of it as God. The word "god" means something a bit different to those who embrace being SBNR. The SBNR tradition has historically referred to God as an impersonal force. While some in traditional religious communities without the directive of sophisticated theological thought conceive of God as a supreme father who rules the universe from a heavenly throne, SBNR (like the mystical element in religion) locates god at the very depths of the self and universe. The ultimate source of things is found within—not beyond—the natural world. The SBNR movement, like traditional religion, thinks of God or this immanent spiritual power as the ultimate source of creation. SBNRers typically view our universe as an evolving universe. They don't think of creation as a "one time only" event. Creation is ongoing. To find a connection with the divine order of things is to be connected to the ultimate source of this ongoing creation. Connecting with the unseen spiritual order of things energizes us to be co-agents of the ongoing creation of the universe.

As many critics of SBNR have pointed out, spirituality cannot be sustainable if receptivity is not matched by purposeful activity. Being SBNR might become a more viable approach to life if it more fully emphasized the fact that we don't simply breathe in. We also breathe out. From a spiritual point of view, becoming inwardly receptive to the inflow of the sacred needs to complete itself by flowing outward toward creative action. Creative action is an action that contributes to the ongoing creation of the universe. It is a healing action. It is a wholeness-making action. It is an action that sustains and nurtures life over time. It is an action that propels every creature to express its highest potentials.

The previous chapter outlined the distinctive traits of a mature spirituality. Among these traits are being dynamic, productive of a consistent morality, and being comprehensive. A spirituality is not sustainable if it is ignorant of all we might know about how best to nurture life over time. Traditional religion conceptualizes God as a heavenly father who demands to be worshipped and obeyed. Individuals are held accountable by being expected to worship in public and adhere strictly to the group's moral code. SBNR, on the other hand, views God as the dimension of depth anywhere and everywhere throughout the universe. Spiritual action, then, isn't about public worship or moral conformity. Spiritual action, instead, is about engaging in wholeness-making action.

A sustainable spirituality must be guided by knowledge gleaned from almost every kind of scientific pursuit. Biological science has much to teach us about how a social species best endures over time. Environmental research has much to offer about how we best achieve the long-term health of a diverse ecosystem. Psychological science can also inform spirituality insofar as it helps us understand the behaviors that lead to robust mental health. What we call developmental psychology has learned much about how we best care for individuals to ensure that they can achieve their highest personal fulfillment. Sociology, too, has learned much about the social structures that best support human fulfillment for all members of society. Economics and political science have also identified those policies that best enrich the lives of an entire nation. It follows that a sustainable spirituality cannot be a lazy spirituality. It must reach out and garner knowledge in a comprehensive fashion. Spirituality begins in becoming inwardly receptive to an unseen order of life. But spirituality completes itself by realizing that our highest good comes from adjusting ourselves harmoniously to an ever-evolving universe. This adjustment is a continuous process. It requires a lifetime of seeking out and absorbing new insights into how we best become agents of the ongoing creation of the universe.

Being SBNR has much to offer a sustainable spirituality of the future. Being SBNR, more than being either wholly secular or being traditionally religious, has the best potential to help us overcome the two main obstacles that stand in the way of sustainable human well-being. Natural selection favored human brains that were (1) designed for personal survival and hence self-centered and (2) designed for short-term satisfaction. Being SBNR has much to entice us into overcoming the first of these obstacles to sustainable modes of living. And, with effort, advocates of SBNR can address the second of these obstacles as well.

The philosopher-psychologist William James examined the first of these obstacles in an essay titled "On a Certain Blindness in Human Beings." The blindness he had in mind "is the blindness with which we are all afflicted in regard to the feelings of creatures and people different from ourselves."[3] James noted that we are practical beings. Each of us is wired to prioritize the actions and duties necessary to our own well-being. As a consequence, we are rarely aware of what James termed "the inner significance" of people or organisms outside our immediate sphere of interest.

James thought that a nature-centered spirituality is the surest route to helping us overcome our blindness to the inner significance of creatures and people different from ourselves. He was very familiar with Emerson's *Nature*. James agreed with Emerson that certain experiences of nature induce awe or wonder. These emotions melt down the walls of egocentrism. They draw us out into closer connection with our surroundings. Awe and wonder lure us into caring about the inner significance of life outside our workaday concerns. The noted ethical theorist Martha Nussbaum has written that the kinds of subjective experiences associated with being SBNR "move distant objects within the circle of a person's scheme of ends ... seeing others as part of one's own circle of concern."[4] In this way, SBNR encourages what might be called an ethics of appreciation (as opposed to an ethics of obedience to ancient social codes). It stimulates wonder at the inner significance of the natural universe in a way that mobilizes our compassion and empathy. SBNR—far more than traditional religion that views nature as a lower form of creation—redraws our world of concern, establishing true mutuality with a wider sphere of life.

James also thought that a nature-centered spirituality can help us surmount the understandable reluctance humans have to seek long-term, rather than short-term, happiness. The human brain is wired for immediate reward. Many of our most pressing problems stem from this fundamental weakness in the human condition: addictions, pollution, obesity, poor educational outcomes, debt, and poor physical fitness. A principal reason we don't behave in sustainable ways is this fundamental unwillingness to sacrifice our personal pleasure in the immediate moment in favor of some more remote, future benefit.

SBNR spirituality has resources that can inspire individuals to forego short-term satisfactions in favor of achieving longer-term goals. It was, once again, William James who saw this unique potential for being SBNR. He noted that traditional religion, despite its teaching that believers need to help create a more just world, has often failed at this task. Its basic image of God has often fostered human complacency. In its most misunderstood form, traditional religion teaches us to rely on faith or prayer, awaiting a transcendent god to intervene to rescue the world from human negligence. Nonreligious humanism is, in James's view, no better in this regard. It can only counsel us to make sacrifices on behalf of future generations of humans. The problem, however, is that most of us simply don't love humans of the future keenly enough. We won't undergo short-term sacrifices for such an abstract or remote future. Being SBNR—like the emotions of awe and wonder—broadens up the infinite perspective. It helps us see our own lives in a much broader metaphysical perspective. This is why, James argued, a spiritual outlook will always incite our deepest passions. When we see ourselves as agents of a divine energy, the infinite perspective opens up. We can see ourselves as co-creators of this evolving universe. And though we may not know precisely where the universe ought to be heading, we know we must act "always for the richer universe, for the good which seems most organizable, most fit to enter into complex combinations, most apt to be a member of a more inclusive whole."[5] We help move the universe forward. We contribute to the realization of the universe's highest potentials.

There are, then, specific ways that being SBNR can give rise to a sustainable spirituality. It might, in fact, hold one of the keys for healing our planet.

NOTES

1 E.O. Wilson, *Sociobiology* (Cambridge, MA: Belknap Press, 1979), p. 55.

2 Catherine Albanese, *A Republic of Mind & Spirit: A Cultural History of American Metaphysical* Religion (New Haven, CT: Yale University Press, 2007).

3 William James, "On a Certain Blindness in Human Beings," in *Talks to Teachers: On Psychology; And to Students on Some of Life's Ideals* (New York, NY: Norton, 1958), p. 149.

4 Martha Nussbaum, *Upheavals of Thought: The Intelligence of Emotions* (Cambridge: Cambridge University Press, 2001), p. 55. For a more extensive discussion of how emotions such as wonder stimulate spirituality and ethical concern, see Robert Fuller, *Wonder: From Emotion to Spirituality* (Chapel Hill, NC: University of North Carolina Press, 2006).

5 William James, "The Moral Philosopher and the Moral Life," in *The Will to Believe* (New York, NY: Dover, 1956), p. 210.

BIBLIOGRAPHY

Albanese, C. *A Republic of Mind & Spirit: A Cultural History of American Metaphysical Religion*. New Haven, CT: Yale University Press, 2007.

Baker, J.O. "A Bounded Affinity Theory of Religion and the Paranormal," *Sociology of Religion*, 77, no. 4 (2016): 334–358.

Fuller, C. ed. *Proceedings of the First International UFO Conference*. New York, NY: Warner Books, 1980.

Fuller, R. *Wonder: From Emotion to Spirituality*. Chapel Hill, NC: University of North Carolina Press, 2006.

James, W. "The Moral Philosopher and the Moral Life," in *The Will to Believe*. New York, NY: Dover, 1956.

James, W. "On a Certain Blindness in Human Beings," in *Talks to Teachers: On Psychology; And to Students on Some of Life's Ideals*. New York, NY: Norton, 1958.

Nussbaum, M. *Upheavals of Thought: The Intelligence of Emotions*. Cambridge, MA: Cambridge University Press, 2001.

Wilson, E.O. *Sociobiology*. Cambridge, MA: Belknap Press, 1979.

7

RETRACING OUR STEPS

VOCABULARY

The words "religious" and "spiritual" really mean the same thing. They refer to humanity's universal desire to harmonize our lives with an unseen order of things. Humans describe this unseen order as sacred, divine, or holy as a way of testifying to their belief that it is qualitatively "higher" than our ordinary, physical reality. Being "religious" or being "spiritual" has traditionally referred to humanity's near-universal quest to find harmony with this higher, unseen order of life.

In recent decades, however, it has become customary to make a distinction between the two words. We use the word "religious" to refer to people who pursue this quest in ways prescribed by a historic tradition. The very word "religion" is derived from the Latin verb *religio*, which means "to bind." Today, we typically use the phrase "being religious" to indicate that we are bound to the beliefs and practices of a specific religious tradition. Being religious means acknowledging that certain books, certain ordained individuals, and certain shared rituals have a special authority over our religious life. Being religious means acknowledging that an established or organized religious heritage has authority over how we seek to harmonize our lives with a divine order of things. The religious quest is thus a quest defined by a particular tradition or institution.

The fact that religious institutions have lost much of their former cultural authority has prompted us to use the words "religious" and "spiritual" a bit differently. It has become

DOI: 10.4324/9781003604259-7

increasingly common to use the word "spiritual"—as opposed to "religious"—to refer to the kinds of religiosity that arise outside established religious traditions. Many individuals find themselves no longer "bound" to the official books, ordained clergy, or mandated rituals of organized religion. They do, however, still desire to understand how we might best harmonize our lives with an unseen or divine order of things. Being spiritual but not religious (SBNR), then, describes those who undertake this spiritual quest in ways that are more private, experiential, and not bound by the traditional dogma found in established religious communities. It is a more experimental, freelance approach to connecting ourselves with a divine reality.

Throughout this book, we have noted that being SBNR is defined both by what it *is against* and what it *is for*. First, it expresses a rejection of traditional religion. It is not bound by any fixed doctrines, rituals, or bureaucracies. Second, being SBNR affirms openness to an unseen (supernatural or metaphysical) order of existence. Unlike those wedded to a strictly scientific or empirical outlook, being SBNR stems from curiosity about what might transcend physical reality. Being SBNR expresses an interest in learning about the kinds of insights or wisdom that have surrounded humanity's historic journeys to explore the highest reaches of the universe.

Individuals who describe themselves as "Spiritual but Not Religious" now comprise somewhere between 22% to 27% of the American population. This percentage is significantly higher among those under 40 years old. Opinion polls show that the number of Canadians who identify as SBNR is slightly higher than is found in the United States, while across all the countries of Western Europe, the percentage of SBNRs is approximately 11%. While debatable, it is possible that identifying oneself as SBNR will characterize an ever-greater segment of modern society in the years ahead.

HISTORICAL ROOTS

While the term "spiritual but not religious" was first used in 1926, its roots go back much further in Western history. There is actually a long tradition of being SBNR. For centuries there have been mystically inclined philosophies that have caught the attention of European readerships. These philosophies, often referred to as Neo-Platonic or Gnostic, have championed the view that humans possess the capacity for inner-connection with "higher" spiritual realities. And, importantly, they have brushed biblical religion to the side and explored metaphysical mysteries independently of institutional constraints. It was, however, in the United States that greater numbers of seekers found a cultural setting most conducive to religious experimentation. A host of metaphysical philosophies sprouted throughout the nineteenth century, helping to popularize new ways of understanding God as an impersonal energy pervading the natural universe. By the late twentieth century, an increasing number of middle-class citizens turned away from established churches. Some had found the churches woefully backward. Biblical religion simply didn't connect with an age defined by scientific knowledge. Others had found the churches oppressive and even abusive. Traditional religious teachings about sexuality and gender became horribly out of touch with many families' lived experience. And others simply found traditional worship services boring. Yet all about them, they could find books, podcasts, seminars, retreats, and lectures encouraging them to venture out on their own spiritual journeys.

There is no question that the SBNR movement was propelled by a number of factors. Among the most prominent of these factors are:

1 *Increasing economic well-being*. Western civilization has enjoyed increasing freedom from poverty, crime, hunger, fear, and existential stress. Alongside of these "freedoms from" have come increasing "freedoms for" education and opportunities to explore ideas generated by those who have lived in diverse cultural settings. All of these weaken institutional religion's ability to bind us to a fixed set of beliefs and practices.
2 *Democracy and capitalism*. SBNR fares best in democratic cultures insofar as the latter valorizes individuality and a consumer approach to religion.

3 *Religious syncretism and spiritual eclecticism.* The latter has been a keynote of American religious history. It has enabled a *combinative* spirit in which people pick and choose from those religious elements that work best for them.
4 *Pluralism.* The advent of multiple religious traditions, aside from that of the Judeo-Christian tradition, added to *combinativeness* by offering the populace a wide assortment of beliefs and practices to utilize in their quest for self-realization.
5 *Influential spokespeople and movements.* Throughout American history, charismatic thinkers like William James and Ralph Waldo Emerson and movements like the transcendentalists, mesmerism, spiritualism, theosophy, New Thought, and Mind Cure evinced the kind of *combinativeness* that filtered into the SBNR mentality.
6 *The counterculture.* The 1950s and 1960s saw the advent of numerous cultural changes that fed directly into the growing popularity of being SBNR. The authorization of alternate sexual lifestyles, communal living, new and revolutionary social spaces (coffee houses, rock concerts), the advent of "missionaries" shopping Eastern religions and techniques, the use of psychedelics, and critical scholarly literature on the "death of God" and patriarchy all served to fuel disillusionment with traditional, organized religion.
7 *Psycho-spirituality.* Multiple new theories about human nature valorizing the deeper spiritual nature of individuals as propagated by theorists like Carl Jung and Abraham Maslow became a feature of the trend towards the psychologization of culture. Stressing inwardness, self-exploration, notably eclectic with regard to religion and seeing in all religions a perennial mystical core, they enhanced the SBNR mindset.
8 *The rise of feminism, the LGBT (Lesbian/Gay/Bi/Trans) movement, and ecological awareness.* The rise of all three attacked the patriarchal power base of institutional religion and its advocacy of a biblically based heteronormativity while resurrecting the value of nature, a long mainstay of being SBNR.

BELIEFS AND PRACTICES

SBNR beliefs and practices range along a wide spectrum. Being SBNR, by definition, means resisting conformity. We have, however, seen that those drawn to being SBNR share four basic attitudes in common:

1 They believe that it is not just the right—but even the duty—of individuals to decide what is true or not true for themselves.
2 They are skeptical of organized religion.
3 They think that the goal of religion should not be about procuring an afterlife; instead, religion should be about enriching this life.
4 They are fascinated by the supernatural and have an abiding interest in topics that suggest the existence of metaphysical realities.

These four attitudes shape the SBNR outlook. They help us understand why those drawn to being SBNR typically hold beliefs about the nature of God, sin, or the afterlife that differ from those associated with biblical religion. Traditional religion has historically portrayed God as a "power over" creation. Religious followers have been asked both to obey and worship their heavenly father. This has, of course, included the notion that followers must submit to religious authorities. In contrast, the SBNR tradition has emphasized thinking about God as an impersonal force that pervades the natural universe. God is thus inwardly available to all who make themselves receptive. In the SBNR worldview, what estranges us from God is not disobedience (sin), but holding on too tightly to our everyday mindset.

Those who are attracted to being SBNR share traditional religion's belief that there is an unseen order (God or the sacred) and that our highest good comes from adjusting ourselves harmoniously thereto. Western religions have traditionally understood this "adjustment" in terms of obedience and worship. Religious practice centers around attendance at formal worship services and following the lead of ordained clergy.

These formal services strike most SBNR adherents as vain repetition: kneeling and rising; reciting ancient creeds, singing hymns, listening to formulaic sermons, etc. SBNR focuses instead on practices that foster inward receptivity. Walking silently through nature, cultivating the emotions of awe and wonder, body movements such as yoga, breathing exercises, divination practices, and introspective psychological techniques are among the practices through which SBNRers seek connection with a higher metaphysical order.

CRITIQUES

There are a number of concerns, issues, and debates about the value of being SBNR. The most common criticism revolves around the degree to which being SBNR fosters "spiritual narcissism." The charge here is that being SBNR encourages self-absorption rather than commitment to a defined community. Most of those who make this charge have ties with organized religion and assume—with little evidence—that attending formal worship services builds strong and supportive communities.

Surveys have shown that there is some merit to this criticism in that traditionally religious people indicate more concern with belonging to a community than do those who align with the SBNR movement. This correlation does not indicate any kind of causation (it is probably the case that this personality difference would exist with or without church membership or SBNR involvement). More importantly, this "criticism" is too sweeping and does not characterize those who profess being SBNR as a whole. One can cite in this regard the early New England Transcendentalists, who made social activism an integral part of their program. Further, some empirical studies show that those who have gone through arduous forms of "humanistic" therapy and its valorization of "peak experiences" become *more* socially engaged. Many SBNR spokespersons go to great lengths to link spirituality with ethical action in relating toward the Earth, animals, and humans of all backgrounds.

A second kind of critique stems from those committed to a thoroughly scientific worldview. In their view, the SBNR movement is chock full of supernatural nonsense. The many New

Age beliefs (auras, reincarnation, astral bodies, astrological influences, the healing value of crystal stones, communication with spirit beings, etc.) that filter into unchurched spirituality strike wholly secular individuals as no different than the ancient dogmas of institutional religion. There is obviously some merit to this criticism, too. Those drawn to the SBNR outlook are typically curious about the unseen orders of the universe. They are thus attracted to any metaphysical idea that promises insight into cosmic mysteries. These ideas are prone to being superficial and faddish.

Being SBNR, like being traditionally religious, relies more on intuitive reasoning than analytic reasoning. It is therefore often characterized by mind/body dualism, supernaturalism, and magical thought. Yet, SBNR's metaphysical tendencies are also capable of eliciting many of humanity's loftiest traits: wonder, ethical idealism, and a vivid sense of our relatedness to the world (including the ecosystem, other human beings, and the ultimate source of the universe). SBNR fosters the range of spiritual sensibilities that seem to form a viable philosophical outlook for humanity's future.

FUTURES

Being SBNR has already become an accepted part of our cultural landscape. Its future is assured, though somewhat dependent on the continued presence of social settings that are relatively free of both existential stress and of religious organizations possessing strong socializing/monitoring abilities. Being SBNR is a viable "third category" alongside being affiliated with an established religious organization or being wholly nonreligious. And, most importantly, it has the potential to blossom into Western culture's most sustainable form of modern spirituality.

SBNR PORTRAITS

A LIFE SHAPED BY WONDER: ENVIRONMENTALIST RACHEL CARSON

It is hard to imagine anyone less likely to become a national celebrity than Rachel Carson (1907–1964). She was shy and soft-spoken. Yet she became the leading voice of the environmental movement that gained momentum in the 1960s. Her *Silent Spring* riveted national attention on the ecological dangers posed by the use of pesticides. The book sold more than half a million copies and stayed on the New York Times best-seller list for 31 weeks. Silent Spring and subsequent publications propelled Carson into the limelight as she found herself the nation's leading advocate of environmental protection.

Rachel Carson grew up in a small town outside Pittsburgh, Pennsylvania. She spent a great deal of her early childhood walking alone beside streams and in the nearby woods. She later recalled that this is when she first developed her love of life and of all living things. On graduation from high school, Rachel entered Pennsylvania College for Women (now Chatham College) to major in literature and writing. Midway through her junior year, however, she changed her major to zoology. She graduated with high honors and decided to pursue a master's degree in marine zoology at the Johns Hopkins University. There were few scientific careers open to women in the 1930s—even those with graduate degrees. Rachel was fortunate to land a civil service position as a writer and editor with the Fish and Wildlife Services. She was initially hired as an assistant aquatic biologist before being promoted to the positions of associate aquatic biologist, aquatic biologist, information specialist, and chief editor of the agency's publications.

Carson worked diligently on an informational article for the Bureau of Fisheries. Her imagination as a creative writer turned the piece into something more akin to poetry than governmental prose. Her supervisor was forced to tell her that the article was unacceptable for governmental use but that she might consider sending it to the *Atlantic Monthly* magazine. She did. The finished work, titled "Undersea," was published in 1937 and inaugurated a career that combined her interests in writing and marine biology. She subsequently resigned from her governmental position and set herself to publishing a number of best-selling books aimed at sharing the very love of life she had first acquired in solitary walks as a child.

Carson was a deliberate writer. She carefully described nature in ways that would evoke a sense of wonder in her readers. She thought it sad that "most of us walk unseeing through the world, unaware alike of its beauties, its wonders, and the strange and sometimes terrible intensity of lives that are being lived about us." She strongly believed that this sense of wonder would incite readers to learn more about the natural universe and, in turn, to care more about it. As she put it,

> once the emotions have been aroused—a sense of the beautiful, the excitement of the new and the unknown, a feeling of sympathy, pity, admiration or love—then we wish for knowledge about the object of our emotional response. Once found, it has lasting meaning.

And, she added, "that the more clearly we can focus our attention of the wonders and realities of the universe about us, the less taste we shall have for destruction."

In midlife, Rachel found herself suddenly faced with raising her deceased niece's son. It was while reflecting on this responsibility that she penned an article for *Woman's Home Companion* titled "Help Your Child to Wonder." This article, later republished as a book titled *A Sense of Wonder*, captured

Carson's vision of how we might help a new generation develop a deeper reverence for life. She began by noting that

> a child's world is fresh and new and beautiful, full of wonder and excitement. It is our misfortune that for most of us that clear-eyed vision, that true instinct for what is beautiful and awe-inspiring, is dimmed and even lost before we reach adulthood.

She then added,

> If I had influence with the good fairy who is supposed to preside over the christening of all children I should ask that her gift to each child in the world be a sense of wonder so indestructible that it would last throughout life, as an unfailing antidote against the boredom and disenchantments of later years, the sterile preoccupation with things that are artificial, the alienation from the sources of our strength.

Carson was well aware that many scoffed at her advocacy for "a sense of wonder." Wonder is, after all, a passive emotion. It is about receptivity to beauty rather than about practical action. Wonder deepens us inwardly, but does nothing to put food on the table or increase our economic well-being. Wonder is content with contemplating what lies just beyond the boundaries of scientific understanding and doesn't inform strategies for worldly success. Yet this is precisely why she believed wonder to be a virtue necessary for the long-term survival of the human species.

What is the value of preserving and strengthening this sense of awe and wonder, this recognition of something beyond the boundaries of human existence? Is the exploration of the natural world just a pleasant way to pass the golden hours of childhood or is there something deeper?

I am sure that there is something much deeper, something lasting and significant. Those who dwell, as scientists or laymen, among the beauties and mysteries of the earth are never alone or weary of life.... Their thoughts can find paths that lead to inner contentment and to renewed excitement in living.

Those who contemplate the beauty of the earth find reserves of strength that will endure as long as life lasts.

Carson didn't expect wonder to lead to the same kinds of truth that we expect from science and technology. As she put it, wonder instead awakens a passion for "some universal truth that lies just beyond our grasp, [a meaning that] haunts and ever eludes us, and in its very pursuit we approach the ultimate mystery of Life itself." Of note is how fully Carson's gentle spirituality differed from that associated with organized religion. Organized religion asks us to view ancient beliefs as fixed truth. Carson, on the other hand, was moved by wonder to open herself to a universe that exceeds our rational grasp. Her spirituality was one of appreciating universal beauty, not reciting ancient creeds.

It is also important to note that Carson's spirituality differed from many of those we associate with being spiritual but not religious (SBNR). She was not especially interested in metaphysical topics (e.g., Asian mystical traditions, meditation practices, subtle energies). Nor did she report having experiences that might be considered in any way paranormal. Hers was a spirituality born of the emotion of wonder—wonder at the natural universe itself (and how such wonder awakens curiosity about whatever unseen order lies beyond our physical senses). Wonder is an emotion that arises when we find ourselves suddenly confronted with something that surpasses rational analysis. It evokes calm contemplation of the "ultimate" source of this inexplicable experience. Rather than prompting to become defensive or concerned for ourselves, wonder draws us out to connect with—and even care for—our surrounding world. These are, of course, the very qualities emanating from Rachel Carson. Her wonder-driven spirituality elicited—and sustained—the very reverence for life that became her abiding legacy.

FROM WALL STREET TO BROADWAY: A SPIRITUAL JOURNEY

Carl Moellenberg has won 14 Tony Awards as a Broadway theatrical producer. Yet none of this came particularly easily. He endured serious challenges along the way. And it required a radical career change after turning 50 years old. He walked away from highly lucrative positions on Wall Street "to create more beauty in the world." And everything in both his personal and professional life soon fell perfectly in place.

This inspiring story is not one about pursuing new business opportunities. It is about an incredible spiritual journey. An extraordinary—indeed paranormal—experience helped him realize that "a divine presence does exist around us if we choose to be sensitive to listening for it." And this divine presence guided him to a wholly new and enriching life.

Carl grew up in a middle-class, Midwestern family. They were not especially religious. His mother had a Protestant (Methodist) background and his father was excommunicated from the Catholic Church for not signing a document saying he would raise his children Catholic. But a few years after college, Carl found himself attending Catholic services in hopes of finding a place where he might "pray about my personal dreams and goals." Attending church brought him a sense of peace and inspired him "to be a kinder person."

But Carl soon found that many of the church's moral teachings went directly counter to his own experience. He had gone on his fair share of dates over the years. Yet well into his career working for Wall Street financial institutions (e.g., Chemical Bank, Morgan Stanley, Goldman Sachs) he became increasingly certain that he was gay. As Carl explains

> being gay is one of one hundred parts that add up to Carl, and a label does not define me ... it was not a choice—it was part of my nature, and I could not change that, God created us and loved all of us as beautiful creatures.

Carl and organized religion were now at odds with one another. He enjoyed the sense of divine presence he experienced during worship services. But the fact remained that "I was worshiping at a place that called me a sinner rather than loving all of God's creatures. I did feel at peace during mass but had the dichotomy of completely disagreeing with many of the church's policies." At about this time, he realized that "a physical church was not necessary for my spiritual goals." Carl does attend mass on occasion. But for the most part, he now forms his own concepts about living spiritually. His quest to gain new spiritual insights led him to explore several alternative healing philosophies predicated on the existence of a "universal energy" called chi (*qi*). As Carl learned, "everything in life is, at core, energy, and learning about energy transfer was an enlightening process." The many seminars and classes that he attended taught him a great deal about this universal energy and how he might transfer this energy into others by volunteering to man a suicide hotline, be a life coach, and help others with stress and pain issues.

Carl's entire life changed in a nanosecond. He was vacationing in France while recovering from seemingly endless complications stemming from treatments related to his recent diagnosis of HIV. He felt fortunate to be alive, given his serious medical condition. Walking alone along the banks of the Loire River, he found himself awash in wonder. The wonder of being alive. The wonder of "the streaks or bolts of reflecting sunlight that were coming toward me almost mystically or supernaturally." He let go. And suddenly he heard a voice: "I realized after a few moments that it was God speaking directly to me." The voice assured him that he should not give up. Despite all odds, he was destined to have a long life ahead of him: "God told me that I was to use that long life to create more beauty in the world. I was here for a reason. I was told that the reason would come to me, and it was in the arts."

No one besides Carl will ever really know what to make of this voice. We didn't experience it. But Carl did. And to him it was vivid, real, and life-transforming. It came out of nowhere. It was wholly unexpected and defied any easy scientific explanation. As he puts it,

> That day on the banks of the Loire was probably the most momentous and illuminating and unbelievable day in my life. I have no doubt it was a conversation with God and that I was steered to a completely new life that brought me joy and renewed passion.

When Carl returned to New York, he resolved to pursue a path of learning how to bring beauty to audiences through theater. He has now produced or co-produced a long list of Broadway hits. Fourteen have earned him Tony Awards. He has worked collaboratively with some of the biggest names (actors, actresses, and directors) in show business. And all of this has flowed directly from that mystical experience along the banks of the Loire River.

Carl Moellenberg's spiritual journey exemplifies many of the principal themes that define being spiritual but not religious. For many years, he valued the peace, serenity, and moral inspiration he experienced while attending formal worship services. Yet over time, he became disenchanted with organized religion. Church doctrines ran counter to his own evolving beliefs. This was particularly the case in regard to church's moral pronouncements about sexuality. Organized religion proclaimed that Carl was a sinner. Every fiber in Carl's body responded to the exact opposite affirmation—the affirmation that God loves all His creations. Then, at a critical moment, Carl had a vivid paranormal experience. His encounter with a divine "voice" was simultaneously eerie and uplifting. It had also had all the features of what philosopher William James called an encounter with a white crow—by which James meant an encounter that establishes beyond personal doubt that there is more to the universe than is detected by our current sciences. Carl became ever-more certain in the existence of an unseen order of life—an order he often describes in terms of a "universal energy" that permeates all of existence. As a consequence, Carl came to view himself as a conduit of this universal energy. His special role was to express this energy through the arts. And, in doing so, he has brought continuous joy into his own life and ours.

SALLY'S INDIVIDUATION

Sally's spiritual journey illustrates the options available to today's seekers. She describes herself as an African-American lesbian. She grew up in Louisiana and was part of a church-going Christian family. Yet rather than feeling nurtured by her family's religious outlook, Sally found it stifling. She was already having difficulty embracing traditional Christian beliefs when she discovered that her sexuality differed from traditional religious views. Sally experienced considerable anxiety and guilt as she feared what others would think if they learned about guilty about her sexual orientation.

When Sally graduated from high school, she moved to the San Francisco Bay area to work for a small start-up company. There she began attending services at The Church for the Fellowship of All Peoples, an interfaith and interracial church that has SBNR overtones. She also experimented with mescalin and yoga in an effort to experience a connection with a higher spiritual reality. Then, in her late 20s, she bumped into an old friend from high school who told her about a retreat that she was leading at the Esalen Institute located down the California coastline at Big Sur. Esalen had been founded decades earlier as a center for all things SBNR. When Sally later looked back at this chance encounter, she deemed it a synchronistic ("meaningful coincidence") event. It was at Esalen that she found that she had an ability to enter into trance states. She describes how, after a long meditation session, she went to an inner place where her thoughts stopped, silence reigned, and she made telepathic contact with angelic personalities. This ecstatic metaphysical experience changed the course of her life. Her friend helped her understand that she had discovered her innate ability to serve as a psychic medium.

With some financial backing, Sally then opened up her own business as a spiritual healer in the Bay area. Through time, she developed a network of relationships with other like-minded seekers. Among those in her loosely knit spiritual community were therapists connected with the San Francisco Jung Center and other practitioners of psycho-spirituality. In advertising her healing service, Sally explicitly states that no one religion has "captured the flag." By this, she means that she embraces people from all walks of life, all religions, all ethnicities, all gender identifications, and all sexual orientations. Sally's therapeutic sessions may include prescribing healing ideas and practices from any number of religious and spiritual paths, depending on the needs of the individual patient. While Sally's advertisements don't actually use the term "SBNR," the whole trajectory of her spiritual path exemplifies all its defining characteristics: unchurched exploration, openness to metaphysical experiences and realities, interest in psycho-spirituality, and a penchant for combinativeness.

FROM CATHOLICISM TO THE SBNR THROUGH THERAPY

As a boy, the young Jeffrey was a simple Midwestern lad from a Catholic family whose parents owned a traditional small-town hardware store. He grew up a Catholic without any real consideration or knowledge of other religious traditions. Later, he admitted that he must have been a repressed young adolescent. He recalls finding sexuality to be dangerous and disgusting. He went on to excel at academics, becoming the valedictorian of his class. He was also skilled at sports at his local high school, becoming the starting quarterback of the team. As time went on, and becoming more religious, he opted for the priesthood in a Catholic seminary, with the possibility of a monastic vocation. At the latter, in reading the works of Teresa of Avila, John of the Cross, and in praying with the Song of Songs, he became interested in the relation of sexuality and the higher saintly life. As the reality of celibacy set in, he became conflicted. Taking the mystical injunction towards asceticism seriously, he lost over 100 pounds and gained a diagnosis of anorexia. These conflicts led him into therapy with a professionally trained psychoanalytic priest at the seminary. There, he came to examine his problems with sexuality. As an adolescent, he had been tormented by a fantasy which consisted of standing with the Virgin Mary beneath a naked Jesus on the cross. Through therapy, he understood the dynamics of the fantasy as revealing a rather pronounced Oedipus conflict and learned how asceticism and sexuality were equated in his unconscious. Gaining much of his weight back during this process, he could admit that therapy had saved his life. But therapy bore fruit in more significant ways. The imagery of other dreams, myths, and visions, which erupted during the course of analysis, made him think of William James and what James called "the More" of the subconscious mind—a "More" that went beyond Freud and Oedipus. To a certain extent, Freud was right, but he was also limited, for something other than an Oedipus complex was being revealed in many of his dreams and visions. This "something more" soon crystallized itself in the following dream:

> The dream involved three presences: myself, a young, attractive maiden dressed in the manner of a Greek or Roman woman, and a winged unicorn whose literally burning body appeared like brilliant black lightning. The maiden said nothing but simply smiled and led me to the edge of what looked like a very deep, very turbulent black sea. Just below the waters burned the fires of a terrifying beautiful winged horse with a single horn coming out of its head. Neither the horn nor the wings were fully grown. The Fire fascinated me – dangerous, dark, and yet filled with light. I instinctively knew that it was my task to get this mysterious being out of the water, and so I entered the waves and tried to pull him up, but to no avail. The scene then shifted and I saw myself as a youth riding naked on the now fully winged and fully horned being into the sky.[1]

This "myth-dream" or "dream-vision" as he called it was far too numinous and mythological to be wholly subsumed as Oedipus. So it is that he, in typical Jungian fashion, searched books in the history of art and religious myths to find similar structural content. He came to realize that the dream was "structured around a profound *coincidentia oppositorium* that would engage me for years to come, that between the mystical and the sexual, or what I would later call the erotic ... if this was sex, it was God's sex."[2] The introspective activity offered through therapy eventually barred him from seeking religious fulfillment in the Catholic church. He simply could not find the solutions to the existential and intellectual problems he was seeking in the resources offered by Christianity. This quandary, as he put it, "exploded my

Catholic world."[3] In all this, he mirrored the spiritual path of Jung. Jung had a fantasy about God defecating on a church cathedral, which led him away from organized religion. In a similar vein, Jeff's impactful dreams and fantasies led him to abandon the seminary for the secular university, where he enrolled as a doctoral student in a department of religion, married, and had children. Detached from a faith commitment to a religious tradition, he came to utilize the tools of academia to extend his researches into the history of mysticism. He became entranced with the modern forms of spirituality, the Esalen Institute (where he was later employed) and concepts of a multiverse (like James). He became convinced that the best way for him to understand his visions and further his spirituality was through writing. He ended up writing numerous books on the relation between sexuality and mysticism. He also wrote in favor of the kind of mindset offered by being SBNR. The backbone of his writing was that the unchurched spiritual path could be facilitated by the daily ritual of exploring, analyzing and then writing about one's own experiences. In this, he was again like Jung, who, in his spiritual autobiography, recounted his numerous encounters with archetypical figures and religious myths and symbols. It was those experiences that came to be the personal material for his later writing, which eventuated in the establishment of an entire psychological system. Similarly, Jeff's own writings became his "path." As he wrote, so too did he discover himself and further his spirituality.

A PLURALISTIC CULTURE

Much like Jung, Jim was the son of a Protestant minister. The family and culture around him was thoroughly Christian. He grew up abroad, as his father's church was involved in missionary activity. He recalls this time as idyllic and insular; a kind of blissful paradise where every need was satisfied. Still a boy, the family returned to the United States to a prominent university town. Jim recalls going to the basement where his father's study was to dress up in his ministerial garb. His father, however, was not adamant about going to church or even talking to the boy about a possible future in the ministry. To the contrary, he held to a theology of grace that was very "hands off." At that time, it was a pluralistic culture, with many different religious traditions represented both at school and at home through visiting friends and acquaintances. So Jim got socialized into multiple religious worldviews and their representatives. Tragedy hit as Jim's father suddenly passed away. A year later, still an adolescent and perhaps due to belated mourning, Jim became interested in transcendental meditation, which he began to practice daily. When he got to college, he decided on philosophy and religion as his major. The college culture was such that he had easy access to hallucinogenic drugs, and he experimented with LSD. While he was cautious about its use, he reported that it gave rise to a whirling tingling sensation, as if someone was applying a jacuzzi to the base of his spine (which he later interpreted as the *kundalini* rising). Such experiences led him to the books of Carlos Castaneda and his psychedelic encounters with the Yaqui Indian shaman Don Juan, which influenced him greatly. Through the recommendation of some college friends, he then decided to try a six-week retreat at a mystical school. It was there that he began to see auras and experienced a kind of divine presence. This series of events led him to realize that the task of life was to (in Christian terms) reform the "imago Dei" within, and that the best way to start that was through therapy. The insights garnered through the latter led him to a nondenominational theological seminary, and the chance encounters with a group of shamans, who disavowed psychedelics but taught him certain introspective mystical practices that led to the awakening of the *kundalini*. This set of experiences led him to reinterpret the Christian tradition along more shamanistic lines, which did not tally with the more orthodox teaching at his seminary. Faced with an intellectual and existential dilemma, Jim decided to forgo a career as a minister in favor of one that favored the arts. In another series of chance events, Jim became involved with the theater and acting. It was then that he moved to Los Angeles, where he made a fairly meager but sustainable existence as an actor, director, and part-time teacher. It was also there that the signature "mystical event" of his life occurred:

> I was asleep in my bed when a weird bluish-white light woke me up. It was still dark outside. Try as a might, I could barely move, although I finally got to a sitting up position. Then I, or my mind, went through a kind of tunnel to another space, which was like a big room with a table of sorts. I was greeted by a light being, lavender in color with big lavender almond shaped eyes, who exuded love and caring. We had a telepathic conversation about my life and where I was headed. Then I was taken through a door and took a tour through what appeared to be a huge mall of some kind, perhaps a ship. I then woke up in my bed in the sitting position, and it was 9 am.

After that, Jim reached out to his contacts in the shaman community. They related to him that this was far from unusual and that they too had had similar experiences. He also reached out to his friends in the Hindu and transcendental meditation community. They sent him some writings on what is known as the "vimana" scriptural literature, which speaks of ancient flying craft that are interdimensional and can take one to various higher heavenly spheres. Jim knew that he needed to do some more research on what had happened. The closest thing he could find to his event were the reports of being abducted by aliens, even if the beings he encountered were not human or the so-called "grays" or reptilians. Faced once again with an intellectual and existential dilemma, Jim started thinking about how to integrate the many religious influences and experiences of his life. How could he integrate his native Christianity, his psychedelic experiences, the shamans he encountered, therapy, his efforts at meditation, and an admittedly very weird seeming alien abduction? Continuing his reading, he came across reports of those who professed to be SBNR. There was much about such narratives that he felt was foreign to his own personal experiences. What he did like was their stress on individualism, individuation (in the Jungian sense), and the pluralistic approach to religion. While he felt a certain bond to his upbringing as a Christian, he also knew that his life trajectory and experiences were such that it put him outside the mainstream of traditional Christian thought. The SBNR was, then the better way of thinking about his almost unique religious path, for it let him be spiritual but in a way not wedded to any mainstream religion but wisdom that he found in multiple ones. As a result, he started frequenting his local Jung Center, where he came across multiple people who had had similar, if not exact, experiences, and with whom he felt he could have honest conversations without being labelled crazy or a heretic. Even more, he felt appreciated and a part of an actual community of like-minded spiritual seekers. He did not give up attending Christian services or continuing to engage in mediative and shamanistic practices. On the contrary, his new community enjoined him to do just that—to continue on his path of self-discovery and spirituality in a way that was unique to him and his spiritual gradient.

NOTES

1 Jeff Kripal, *Roads of Excess, Palaces of Wisdom: Eroticism and Reflexivity in the Study of Mysticism* (Chicago, IL: The University of Chicago Press, 2001), pp. 92–93.
2 Jeff Kripal, *Roads of Excess, Palaces of Wisdom: Eroticism and Reflexivity in the Study of Mysticism* (Chicago, IL: The University of Chicago Press, 2001), p. 93.
3 Jeff Kripal, *Roads of Excess, Palaces of Wisdom: Eroticism and Reflexivity in the Study of Mysticism* (Chicago, IL: The University of Chicago Press, 2001), pp. 94–95.

BIBLIOGRAPHY

Carson, R. *A Sense of Wonder*. New York, NY: Harper & Row, 1956.
Carson, R. *Silent Spring*. Boston, MA: Houghton Mifflin, 1962.
Fuller, R. *Wonder: From Emotion to Spirituality*. Chapel Hill, NC: University of North Carolina Press, 2006.
Kripal, J.J. *Roads of Excess, Palaces of Wisdom: Eroticism and Reflexivity in the Study of Mysticism*. Chicago, IL: The University of Chicago Press, 2001.
Moellenberg, C. *Carl Moellenberg's Story: Broadway and Spirituality as a Path to Survival*. Irvington, NY: Imagine & Wonder Books, 2022.

APPENDIX

For further reading

Bach, R. *Jonathan Livingston Seagull.* New York, NY: Macmillan, 1970.

This book is an allegorical fable which follows the life of a seagull named Jonathan. The fable is "really" about the virtues of nonconformity, of seeking one's destiny for oneself, of self-discovery, of freedom, and of returning to help others in their own quest for authenticity. Throughout the story, one can find multiple elements of the human potential movement, of Jung's notion of individuation, and of the stress on spirituality that is endemic to the spiritual but not religious (SBNR) movement.

Bender, C. *The New Metaphysicals: Spirituality and the American Religious Imagination.* Chicago, IL: The University of Chicago Press, 2010.

This book is a sociological and ethnographic study which details the beliefs and practices of several spiritual seekers in the Cambridge, Massachusetts area. Particularly valuable for the multiple case histories she recounts and how significant spiritual experiences shaped the lives of those practitioners seeking transcendence in the modern world. Bender shows how such experiences are interpreted, how they draw on cultural resources going back well into the past, and how they impact the lives of the seekers.

Carrette, J. and R. King, *Selling Spirituality.* New York, NY: Routledge, 2005.

This book is often framed as the *de facto* treatment of SBNR. Its stresses how the SBNR is really about narcissism. Their genealogy of being SBNR siphons through two major historical movements: (1) that which echoes the enlightenment stress on the privatization of religion and focus on the individual, and (2) the subsequent twentieth-century "corporatization of spirituality" in which neoliberalism has tailored individual desires for self-fulfillment for the purpose of continuously reproducing the capitalistic ethos of growth, industrial efficiency, profitability, and success. They see psychology as a major cultural strand in the formation of both modern spirituality and its myopic focus on the individual. In particular, it is James, who both privatized and democratized religious experience, and then Maslow and his "growth"-oriented humanistic psychology—one in which a person's basic needs and the valorization of peak experiences reflects, supports, and reproduces neoliberal capitalism—that dot their argument.

Castaneda, C. *A Separate Reality*. New York, NY: Simon & Schuster, 1971.

This is the second in a series of books about Castaneda's relationship with the Yaqui Indian shaman Don Juan. In it, he details his multiple inner journeys as facilitated by various psychotropic plants, especially peyote, and the entirely new way of seeing reality that was the end product. In valorizing indigenous cultures, mind altering substances, and the life and connectivity of nature, Castaneda's books had a profound effect on the emergence of nontraditional ways of formulating one's spiritual journey.

Chandler, S. "The Social Ethic of Religiously Unaffiliated Spirituality," *Religious Compass*, 2, no. 2 (2008): 240–256. Doi:10.1111/j.1749-8171.2007.00059.x

By surveying extant literature on the SBNR, which portrays it as essentially narcissistic, vacuous, the product of late modernity, and incapable of contributing to culture, Chandler argues the contrary. She points out that the empirical data does not support such narratives; that many studies show a more positive correlation between being SBNR and civic engagement; and that a more developed view of being SBNR supports the narrative that modern spirituality can be framed as socially engaged and productive.

Dillard, A. *Pilgrim at Tinker Creek*. New York, NY: Harper, 1974.

This book is a work of creative nonfiction that describes the author's reflections upon her immersion in the life of nature as found in and around Tinker Creek in the Blue Ridge Mountains. Described as a kind theologizing of nature and the divine and at attempt to reconcile evil with the presence of the divine, the book investigates the multiple aspects of nature; the good, the bad, the incomprehensible, the sinister, the glory. Dillard herself notes that one can find in the book the *via positiva*, which emphasizes the glory and beauty of creation, and the *via negativa*, which ends in a kind of nothing. It is a testament to the kind of profound impact of nature on the SBNR mindset which stretches back to Thoreau's *Walden* and the Transcendentalist movement.

Ecklund, E. and D. Di, "Global Spirituality Among Scientists," in W.B. Parsons ed., *Being Spiritual but Not Religious: Past, Present, Future(s)*. New York, NY: Routledge 2018, pp. 163–178.

This invaluable essay begins the difficult process of ascertaining to what extent (if at all) being SBNR is a global phenomenon. A close analysis of scientists' narratives confirms that there are indeed scientists who claim to be SBNR across the four national contexts surveyed (Taiwan, France, the U.S.A, and the U.K.) but that culture influences the way in which they construct and hence understand spirituality. In Taiwan, spirituality refers to the continuation of Taiwanese traditions through their occasional practice of folk religions; in France counterparts, the negation of supernatural meaning and the furtherance of humanism; in the U.K. and the U.S.A constructing an alternative value system without affiliating with a specific religious tradition. The paper highlights the role of history and culture in contextualizing spirituality, calls for more global ethnographic research, and draws attention to the hurdles required to begin a dialogue about comparative utility.

Ellwood, R. *The Fifties Spiritual Marketplace: American Religion in a Decade of Conflict*. New Brunswick, NJ: Rutgers University Press, 1997.

In addition to describing the relationship between Protestant and Catholic denominations in a decade with record high weekly attendance, Ellwood provides keen insight into the underground forms of Fifties religiosity. He provides helpful analyses of the rise of unconventional spiritualities such as "Beat" Zen, UFO contactees, Thomas Merton monasticism, and the Joseph Campbell/Carl Jung revival of mythology.

Ellwood, R. *The Sixties Spiritual Awakening: American Religion Moving from Modern to Post Modern*. New Brunswick, NJ: Rutgers University Press, 1994.

The 1960s were many things to many people: political clashes over the Vietnam War, rock music, drugs, and extremist lifestyles. But historian

Robert Ellwood reminds us that this decade was above all about new kinds of spirituality. He chronicles the important shift in the character of American religion, from an institutionally based to a more subjective experience of the divine.

Fitzpatrick, S. and W.B. Parsons, "The Triumph of the Therapeutic and Being SBNR," in W.B. Parsons ed., *Being Spiritual but Not Religious: Past, Present, Future(s)*. New York, NY: Routledge 2018, pp. 30–44.

The cultural soup we now inhabit takes for granted a spiritual search guided by psychological terms such as self-actualization, individuation, and peak experiences. This book chapter traces how that came to be while providing empirical evidence which challenges the claim, most persuasively argued in Carrette and King's *Selling Spirituality*, that that such spaces have primarily resulted in a form of spiritual narcissism.

Fuller, R. *Alternative Medicine and American Religious Life*. New York, NY: Oxford University Press, 1989.

A high percentage of the alternative medical systems that have gained popular followings do so by offering spiritual philosophies that resonate with America's SBNR traditions. This book traces the metaphysical dimensions of such unorthodox medical systems as homeopathy, hydropathy, mesmerism, osteopathy, chiropractic, crystal healing, sundry massage therapies such as rolfing or shiatsu, and Alcoholics Anonymous.

Fuller, R. *Spiritual, But Not Religious: Understanding Unchurched America*. New York, NY: Oxford University Press, 2001.

This book traces the historical development of unchurched spirituality from the mid-nineteenth century, when audiences responded enthusiastically to new philosophies such as Transcendentalism, right up to the current interest in meditation, channeling, divination, and psychospiritualities. Far from being flighty or narcissistic as the popular press often makes them out to be, individuals drawn to the SBNR movement often embrace a mature and dynamic set of basic beliefs. They focus on inner sources of spirituality, emphasize this world rather than the afterlife, believe in the mind's untapped powers, insist on equality between genders, sexualities, or races, and affirm a fundamental unity between science and religion.

Fuller, R. *Wonder: From Emotion to Spirituality*. Chapel Hill, NC: University of North Carolina Press, 2006.

This book argues that the emotion of wonder is a principal source of humanity's belief in the existence of an unseen order of life. Like no other emotion, wonder prompts us to pause, admire, and open our hearts and minds. The book provides overviews of the scientific study of emotion and the characteristics of wonder-driven cognition. Chapters on such "exemplars of wonder" as John Muir, William James, and Rachel Carson illustrate wonder's role in personal spirituality.

Fuller, R. and W.B. Parsons "Spiritual but Not Religious: A Brief Introduction," in W.B. Parsons, ed., *Being Spiritual but Not Religious: Past, Present, Future(s)*. New York, NY: Routledge, 2018, pp. 15–29.

This book is a short, informative summary of the historical roots and cultural influences that lie behind the emergence of being SBNR. The essay begins by tracing the genealogy of the "churched" terms spirituality and mysticism from their historical roots in early Greek and Christian culture to the ministrations of liberal Protestant thought and Transcendentalism in the eighteenth and nineteenth centuries to the introduction of the term "SBNR" in the early twentieth century. It then surveys various cultural movements (i.e., early American strands; the metaphysical "isms"; countercultural currents) that helped to further define the term. Finally, it settles on studies concerning its contemporary demographics.

Hammarskjöld, D. *Markings*, translated by L. Sjöberg and W.H. Auden. New York, NY: Alfred A. Knopf, 1964.

From the pen of the former Secretary-General of the United Nations, this book was published posthumously. It consists of a collection of poems, personal reflections on spirituality, and journal entries. It reveals how he dealt with the struggles of his personal faith, public service, and what it means to be human. In particular, the book shows how he connected his private spirituality to his active social service. His view was that holiness cannot dispense with action and service to others.

Hesse, H. *Siddhartha*. New York, NY: New Directions, 1951.

This is a classic philosophical novel work which details the journey of a young spiritual seeker. Resonating through history and commensurate with the modern SBNR mentality, Hesse details the vicissitudes of life "in the world," with all of its allures (fame, sex, riches), their inevitable inability to proffer true happiness, the subsequent turn within, and the achievement of liberation. The book was dedicated to Romain Rolland, who was the man responsible for asking Sigmund Freud to analyze the famous "oceanic feeling," and who advocated for a "universal science-religion."

Huxley, A. *The Doors of Perception*. San Francisco, CA: Harper & Row, 1954.

Written in 1954 during a renaissance of interest in psychedelic drugs, this book can rightly be characterized as a classic. In it, Huxley describes his experiences with mescaline, a psychedelic found in peyote. He promotes the idea that there exists a perennial core to all religious traditions; that the core consists of mystical insight; and that mescaline and other psychedelics are the royal road to producing a similar experience in all individuals. Very readable and short, this book subsequently became a virtual unchurched bible for those seeking to access the divine through psychedelics.

Jung, C. *Memories, Dreams, Reflections*. New York, NY: Vintage, 1989.

This book is Jung's spiritual autobiography. Focusing at first on his childhood, he details his initial wish to follow in the footsteps of his father, who was a Protestant minister. He then goes on to summarize the pivotal events (i.e., a disillusioning first communion experience; a fantasy where God destroys the church in favor of an unchurched way of approaching the divine) which led him away from the church and into psychiatry, to Freud, and to psychoanalysis. In a pivotal chapter titled "confrontation with the unconscious," he describes another series of mystical encounters (and later in the book a near-death experience) with various figures which became the experiential basis for the formulation of his archetypical psychology. He also indicates how this new psychology can be viewed as the key to the myths and symbols of the world's religious traditions (hence a psycho-spirituality).

Kelly, J.J. "Rogue Mystics: The Ecology of Cosmic Consciousness," in W.B. Parsons ed., *Being Spiritual but Not Religious: Past, Present, Future(s)*. New York, NY: Routledge 2018, pp. 181–199.

Kelly starts by unpacking the idea of cosmic consciousness as it developed in the late nineteenth century in the writings of Walt Whitman, R.M. Bucke, and Edward Carpenter. Drawing on key texts of these intellectuals, he suggests their conception of cosmic consciousness presents an alternative interpretation of spiritual subjectivity that can be characterized as "nondualistic," "embodied," and "socially-engaged." Then, drawing on this "cosmic" interpretation of spiritual subjectivity as outlined by these "rogue mystics," he argues for a contemporary and future-oriented SBNR understanding of spiritual ecology and the role it can play in vitalizing political action.

Kripal, J.J. *Esalen: America and the Religion of No Religion.* Chicago, IL: The University of Chicago Press, 2007.

This book is a history of the origins, development, and practices of a central SBNR institution. It shows how Esalen became at the forefront of the human potential movement and the major therapeutic retreat center for those seeking to combine Western psychology with mystical traditions in a way that rejected dogmatism, religious hierarchies, and religious particularism.

Lofton, K. *Oprah: The Gospel of an Icon.* Berkeley, CA: University of California Press, 2011.

Lofton's book frames Oprah as advocating a form of spiritual consumerism complete with an idealized spiritual figure (Oprah herself) who promotes books, practices, therapies, and a secular spiritual gospel designed to foster growth, renewal, and self-transformation. Lofton sees Oprah as a uniquely American product in its appeal to individualism, wealth and, at times, narcissism, turning spirituality into a marketable product.

Mercadante, L. *Belief without Borders: Inside the Minds of the Spiritual but Not Religious.* New York, NY: Oxford University Press, 2014.

This book is a project in the theology of culture, which brings into dialogue the SBNR mindset with the metaphysical and ethical doctrines of Christianity. It does so by drawing on interviews with hundreds of self-identified SBNRs concerning the "big questions" many humans ponder: Are there any transcendent powers greater than myself? What does it mean to be human? Does community help or hinder spiritual growth? Is there an afterlife? These questions also translate into the issues of transcendence/immanence (God), theological anthropology, ecclesiology, and eschatology. The interviewee responses analyzed in this research add surprising features to the information gathered by various social science surveys over the years.

Miller, L. *The Awakened Brain*. New York, NY: Penguin, 2022.

This is one of the major, readable books on the new emerging neuroscience of spirituality. Miller argues that there is a spiritual human capacity which is not the province of any particular religion but universal, unchurched, and capable of being scientifically analyzed. She shows how multiple activities, such as meditation, prayer, yoga, and communing with nature, activate and develop one's innate spiritual human capacity, helping to ward off depression and facilitate bonds with others and community.

Parsons, W.B. "Religion in the 21st Century: Whither Being Spiritual but Not Religious," *CR: The New Centennial Review*, 22, no. 2 (2022): 79–110.

This book traces the historical development of terms such as mysticism and spirituality, segueing to the SBNR and its possible future. That future involves the increase of empathy in human beings and a new metaphysic that takes into account the coming recognition of extraterrestrial life. He notes how humans have progressed from flat earth theory, from geocentrism to heliocentrism, and the notion of evolution. The next step, which we are now in the middle of, is acknowledging the reality of exoplanets and intelligent life elsewhere. Parsons sifts through the empirical, scientific literature on unidentified anomalous objects, the reports of the "experiencers," and scholarly literature on evidence within the traditions of nonhuman life to argue how the SBNR is equipped to deal with this coming reality.

Parsons, W.B. "Mysticism: An Overview," in J. Barton, ed., *Oxford Research Encyclopedia of Religion*. New York, NY: Oxford University Press, 2019.

This book is a helpful guide to the genealogy of the terms mysticism and spirituality from their classic, traditional, institutional origins and meanings to the more unchurched meaning found in the SBNR. Summarizes the emergence of modern spirituality, the coining of the term "SBNR," and the origin and development of psycho-spiritualities.

Pevateaux, C. "Being Spiritual but Not Hierarchical," in W.B. Parsons ed., *Being Spiritual but Not Religious: Past, Present, Future(s)*. New York, NY: Routledge, 2018, pp. 236–252.

Pevateaux's aim is to show how being SBNR alleviates the more traditional religious stress on oppressive hierarchies. He argues that a motivating factor for being SBNR lies in part because of their rejection of such churched structures. Indeed, of all systems of human cultures, those we deem religious perhaps fare the worst with respect to hierarchical oppression—of women and people of color, of nonhuman animals, and of the environment. The question at the heart of this essay is how a move away from oppressive hierarchies of all kinds towards a more just and interconnected egalitarianism can be a central motif of those who proclaim being SBNR.

Redfield, J. *The Celestine Prophecy*. New York, NY: Warner, 1993.

This book is a story about a spiritual awakening and development centered around an ancient, mysterious manuscript in Peru which contains insights, prophecies, and teachings from a lost Celestine civilization. Embarking upon a quest to find and integrate the wisdom contained in the manuscript, the protagonist encounters governmental and religious forces determined to suppress its message of spiritual liberation. The wisdom pushes the notion that the universe is an energy vortex which responds to our spiritual needs, sending us meaningful coincidences, intuitions, and even mystical experiences designed to further individual and social transformation. It is, then, an instance of the SBNR quest for the kind of metaphysical combinativeness which goes beyond both materialism and the more austere and conservative nature of traditional church dogmatism.

Schmidt, L. *Restless Souls: The Making of American Spirituality*. San Francisco, CA: Harper, 2005.

Schmidt's book *Restless Souls* is a counter to the argument of *Selling Spirituality* in that it reminds us that being SBNR has taken many forms, ranging back well over a century to the creative self-expression, rugged individualism, and social activism of members of the Transcendentalist movement such as Emerson, Thoreau, and Margaret Fuller. Schmidt uses this more socially engaged, transformational understanding of the roots of being SBNR to critique Carrette and King's one-dimensional focus on its complicity with neoliberal capitalism.

Schmidt, M. *In Search of the Spirit: American Spirituality*. Charlottesville, VA: University of Virginia Press, 2019.

This is a series with multiple books dedicated to exploring the origins and development of spirituality in America. Its stated aim (from its website) is to publish "histories, ethnographies, biographies, and critical editions designed to deepen understanding of the varied ways that Americans have imagined spirituality, past and present." As such, the series advances new critical perspectives on how religious norms, practices, and institutions—including the very labeling of "religion" and "spirituality"—have been thrashed out in American culture.

Watts, G. *The Spiritual Turn*. New York, NY: Oxford University Press, 2022.

This book is a sociological, ethnographic, and historical study of what Galen calls "the religion of the heart" understood as a form of romantic liberal religiosity and in which SBNR can fit. He argues that this form of religion has roots well into the American past and can be found in multiple forms today. To that end, he provides on-site ethnographic analyses of three institutions: the New Life Fellowship, C3 Toronto, and an offshoot of Toastmasters International. His research showed that there are multiple themes that pervade such places, including forms of "God" as immanent and a stress on self-realization, individualism, and the sacredness of individual liberty. Galen rejects a turn to Biblical fundamentalism and, while acknowledging the pitfalls of the SBNR mentality, sees it as the best way forward.

White, C. *Other Worlds: Spirituality and the Search for Invisible Dimensions*. Cambridge, MA: Harvard University Press, 2018.

Pitched to the educated layperson as well as the interested scholar, White presents an intellectual history of the origins and development of how notions of invisible dimensions came to be so firmly a part of our culture. He takes us through a host of originative figures, ranging from mathematicians, physicists, and literary figures to parapsychologists, television producers and artists, as well as a variety of familiar social groups, movements, and cultural phenomena to their creative expression in entangled social spaces, their multiple eddies of influence on each other and subsequent others, their impact on cultural constructions of gender and race and, most specifically, the religious imagination, understood as a veritable "scientific supernatural." He describes a modern democratization of mysticism, the beginning of a scientific supernatural, and dimensional framings of pivotal concepts such as the Incarnation and Resurrection. White also goes beyond the originative figures to show how their ideas came to affect a wide assortment of pivotal twentieth-century figures and movements, invariably infecting social media (e.g., Marshall McLuhan, Terence McKenna, Philip Dick, C.S. Lewis; Lewis Carroll; theosophy; psycho-spirituality; television; and movies). It is valuable for a scholarly treatment of the kind of metaphysical ideas found in the SBNR.

Wuthnow, R. *After the Baby Boomers: How Twenty- and Thirty-Somethings are Shaping the Future of American Religion.* Princeton, NJ: Princeton University Press, 2007.

This book is a wide-ranging sociological study that examines the religious trends in American society. Wuthnow focuses on how the growth in churched religion is declining and how many post-baby boomers prefer a more individualistic approach to spirituality. He also explores the impact of the Internet, virtual churches, and the rise of megachurches.

PODCASTS

***Spiritual but Not Religious* (Jill Dominguez). https://www.spiritualbnr.org/podcast**

Multiple episodes consisting of interviews with prominent people, meditations and practices, and inquiries into religious texts that facilitate the SBNR mindset.

***Sacred Inclusion Network* (Angelo John Lewis, Cindy Franklin, Rene Molencamp). https://sacredinclusion.com/audio/**

An internationally based site delving into all matters spiritual designed to facilitate the growth of knowledge and community. Includes an interview with the sociologist Sibohan Chandler about the nature of the SBNR.

***On Being* (with Krista Tippett). https://onbeing.org/series/podcast/**

Devoted to spiritual wisdom and inquiry, social healing, science, and poetry. Includes a 20-year archive with interviews with such luminaries as Desmond Tutu, Mary Oliver, Thich Nhat Hanh.

INDEX

Note: Page numbers followed by "n" refer to end notes.

the Absolute 7
African-American lesbian 142–144
After the Baby Boomers: How Twenty- and Thirty-Somethings are Shaping the Future of American Religion (Wuthnow) 160
agnostics 115
Aizenstat, S. 101
Alcoholics Anonymous 10–12
Alpert, R.: SBNR advocacy 54–55
Alternative Medicine and American Religious Life (Fuller) 153
The Anaesthetic Revelation and the Gist of Philosophy (Blood) 51
analytic reasoning 84
animal magnetism 33
archetypal activism 101
Aristotle 103
asceticism 49, 144
Asian Exclusion Act of 1924 43
atheist 115
autonomous/healthy narcissism 101
The Awakened Brain (Miller) 157
awe and wonder 77, 85, 119, 126–127, 134, 138
Bach, R. 150
Barton, J. 157
"Being Spiritual but Not Hierarchical" (Pevateaux) 157–158
Being Spiritual but Not Religious: Past, Present, Future(s) (Parsons) 152–153, 154, 155–156, 157–158
Belief without Borders: Inside the Minds of the Spiritual but not Religious (Mercadante) 156
beliefs/attitudes in SBNR 133–134; choosing for oneself 68–69; fascination with metaphysical experiences and realities 73–76; focusing on afterlife *vs.* focusing on this life 70–73; skepticism toward organized religion 69–70
Bellah, R. 96, 107
Bender, C. 150
Beyond God the Father (Daly) 58
the Bible 11, 18, 23, 26, 30, 45, 71, 94
Big Five personality traits 82
Bill W. 10–12
Blake, W. 54
Blavatsky, H. 37–38
Blood, P. 51

Boyer, L. 7
Brave New World (Huxley) 53
Bucke, R. M. 48–49
Buddhism 37, 38, 54

cafeteria Catholics 109
Campbell, J. 48
The Care of the Soul (Moore) 48
Carrette, J. 98–100, 150–151
Carson, C. 136–139
Castaneda, C. 25, 151
The Celestine Prophecy (Redfield) 158
chakras (spiritual centers) 38
Chandler, S. 151
Christianity 1, 7, 58, 94, 105–106; Bishop of Rome 19; God, expressions of 72; hierarchical authority 19; historical core of 71; Protestant Christian organizations 19; socializing individuals 18–19
The Church and the Second Sex (Daly) 57
Church for the Fellowship of all Peoples, San Francisco 99
classical mysticism 95
cognitive science 83
collective unconscious 48
collectivism 81
colonial-era healing practices 22
combinativeness 14, 62–63, 88, 120, 122
cosmic consciousness 49, 53
counter-culture, 1950–1970 41–45, 132; college classrooms 45; counseling sessions 44; Eastern religions, acceptance and popularity of 42–44; psychotherapy 44; public art 45
criticisms 134–135; assessment of 105–111; contrary view 99–103; secular critiques of 103–105; spiritual narcissism and SBNR 96–99; traditional religion's problems with 93–96
cultural criticism hypothesis 100
cultural wisdom 42
The Culture of Narcissism (Lasch) 99

Dalai Lama 43
Daly, M. 57–60; theological education 57
Dass, R. 55
Davis, A. J. 36
de-idealization 87
Dern, L. 4
"developmental infrastructure" of belief 87
Dharmapala, Anagarika 43
Di, D. 16n1, 152
Dillard, A. 151–152
Dillon, M. 100
divination practices 23, 79, 134
divine messages 117
divine presence 28, 73, 95, 106, 140, 147
divine reality 130
The Doors of Perception (Huxley) 155
drug-driven illuminations: LSD-25 53, 55; mescaline 54, 55; metaphysical 53, 56

Eastern religions, acceptance and popularity of 42
Eastern spirituality 43–44
Ecklund, E. 16n1, 152
ecological awareness 61, 132
ecological spirituality 61
Eddy, M. B. 35
ego, dissolution of 55
Ellwood, R. 152
Emerson, R. W. 9, 13, 27–32, 47, 50, 70, 73, 99, 100, 132; education 27–28; God's presence, vision of 28–29; metaphysical correspondence, principle of 31, 38;

multidimensional nature of the universe, notion of 31; Over-Soul, metaphor of 30; spirituality 28; walking silently in nature 28–29, 77
Enlightened (HBO TV series) 4
entheogens 14, 53–56
Esalen: America and the Religion of No Religion (Kripal) 156
Esalen Institute 4, 43, 108, 143, 146
Evans, W. F. 35

feminist spirituality 58–59
The Fifties Spiritual Marketplace: American Religion in a Decade of Conflict (Ellwood) 152
Fitzpatrick, S. 153
Foucault, M. 98
Franklin, B. 20
Freud, S. 48, 88, 117–118, 145
Fuller, M. 9, 99, 100
Fuller, R. 153–154

Gaia hypothesis 61
Ginsberg, A. 54
"Global Spirituality Among Scientists" (Ecklund and Di) 152
God 124; as "Be-ing" 58; as the collective unconscious 11; presence in natural world 28–29
God of the Bible 26, 30
groupthink 21

Hammarskjöld, D. 154
Hanegraaff, W. 22
Harvard Medical School 44
Harvard Psychedelic Drug Research Project 54
healthy narcissism 106–107
Hesse, H. 154–155
Hinduism 37, 38, 54
hippie movement 42, 109
Hofmann, A. 53
Horton, M. 22
humanistic psychology 46, 48, 98
Huxley, A. 54, 155
Huxley, T. 53–54; mescaline-enhanced perception 54

individualism 4, 50, 81–83
individualization theory 120–121
individuation 89–90, 142–144; definition of 89
Industrial Revolution 21
inner-worldly asceticism 49
inner-worldly mysticism 49, 50
In Search of the Spirit: American Spirituality (Schmidt) 158–9
institutional religion 3–4, 21; historical dominance of 18–20
introspection 101, 134, 145, 147
In Tune with the Infinite (Trine) 35
inward receptivity 31, 134
Isis Unveiled (Blavatsky) 37
Islam 18, 94

James Sr., H. 50
James, W. 6, 8, 11–12, 47, 98, 110, 126, 132; metaphysical illumination 51–52; psychedelic illumination, discovery of 53; SBNR tradition, contributions to 50–53; "searching for white crows" 74–75; spiritual restlessness 51
Jefferson, T. 20
Jewish population in the United States 24
Jonathan Livingston Seagull (Bach) 150
Judaism 18, 94; principal focus of 71
Jung, C. 11, 48, 101, 132, 146, 155; Cathedral fantasy 86, 87; Christian doctrines, rejection

of 11; individuation 89–90; synchronicity, notion of 90
Jung Center of Houston 102
Jungian social service 102

Kelly, J. J. 155–156
King, R. 98–100, 150–151
Kripal, J. J. 156
kundalini, awakening of 147

Larson, S. 97
Lasch, C. 99
Leary, T. 54–55
Lesbian/Gay/Bi/Queer/Trans (LGBQT) movement 56, 60–61, 132
liberal-leaning religious groups 68
Lofton, K. 99, 156
Lovelock, J. 61
LSD-25 53, 55, 147

Mad Men (AMC TV series) 4
mahatmas 37–38
Markings (Hammarskjöld) 154
Marriage of Heaven and Hell (Blake) 54
Marx, K. 98
Maslow, A. 46, 47, 98, 132
meditation 38; mindfulness meditation 78
Memories, Dreams, Reflections (Jung) 86, 155
Mercadante, L. 103, 156
mescaline 54, 55
Mesmer, F. A. 33
mesmerism 32–34, 33, 36–37, 132, 153
metaphysical correspondence, principle of 31, 38
metaphysical curiosity 32–39, 74
Miller, L. 157
Mind Cure philosophy 34–35, 132
Moellenberg, C. 139–142
Moore, T. 48
moral realism 104
"the More" of subconscious mind 145
mysticism 7–8, 95–96, 159
"Mysticism: An Overview" (Parsons) 157
mystikos 7

narcissism: healthy and unhealthy 106–107; spiritual 96–99, 134
Narcissistic Personality Inventory (NPI) 106
Native Americans, religiosity of 25
Nature (Emerson) 28, 29, 73, 126
Neo-Paganism 60
The New Metaphysicals: Spirituality and the American Religious Imagination (Bender) 150
New Thought movement 35, 110, 132
Nietzsche, F. 43
nonbelievers 21
nonreligious 115–116; agnostics 115; atheist 115; secularization theory 115
nonreligious humanism 127
Nussbaum, M. 126

occult practices 24
Oedipus complex 144–145
Olcott, H. S. 37, 43
Oprah 99
Oprah: The Gospel of an Icon (Lofton) 156
Orthodox Christianity 19
other-worldly asceticism 49
other-worldly mysticism 49, 50
Other Worlds: Spirituality and the Search for Invisible Dimensions (White) 159
Otto, R. 47
Over-Soul, metaphor of 30
Oxford Research Encyclopedia of Religion (Barton) 157

Pacifica Graduate Institute 101
Pagans 60–61

Paine, T. 20
Palmer, D.D. 32
paranormal events/experiences 48, 74–75, 96, 109
Parsons, W. B. 152, 154, 157
peak experiences 46–47, 98
Peck, M. S. 97
perennialism 38, 54
Perennial Philosophy (Huxley) 54
petitionary prayer 106
Pevateaux, C. 157–158
Pilgrim at Tinker Creek (Dillard) 151–152
Piper, L. 75
Plato 41
pluralism 50, 68, 132
pluralistic culture 146–149
power from within 60, 61
"powow" healing system 23–24
practices in SBNR 76–80, 133–134; body work, forms of 78–79; divination practices 79; meditation 78; psycho-spiritualities 78; sitting quietly 79; walking silently in nature 77–78; wear jewelry/display tattoos 80
The Psychedelic Experience (Leary, Dass, and Metzner) 55
Psychedelic Prayers (Leary) 55
psychedelics 53–55; psychedelic illumination 53–54
psychological traits, SBNR individuals 84–85
psychology 45–46; humanistic psychology 46, 48, 98; and spirituality 48
psycho-spirituality 45–50, 78, 86, 89, 132; cosmic consciousness 49; hierarchy of human needs 46; pastoral counseling 45; peak experiences 46–47; self-actualization 46
psychotherapy 44

Quimby, P. P.: Mind Cure philosophy 34–35

Redfield, J. 158
Reform Judaism 24, 68
reincarnation 38, 39, 56, 71, 76
religion 5–6, 118–119; authentic religion 8; goal of 89; organized religion 42, 47; skepticism toward organized religion 69–70; submission and obedience to God 70, 94; truth of 29; "truth" of 11; ultimate truth of 38; word origin 129
"Religion in the 21st Century: Whither Being Spiritual but Not Religious" (Parsons) 157
religiosity: being nonreligious 2, 115–116; being religious 2, 6, 68, 116–121, 129; being SBNR 3–5, 12–13, 16n1, 67–70, 121–123 (*see also* beliefs/attitudes in SBNR; practices in SBNR)
religious impulses 118
religious syncretism 132
Restless Souls: The Making of American Spirituality (Schmidt) 100, 158
Ripley, G. 29, 69
The Road Less Travelled (Peck) 97
"Rogue Mystics: The Ecology of Cosmic Consciousness" (Kelly) 155–156
Rolland, R. 43
Roman Catholicism 19
Roof, W. C. 55–56
Rowland, H. 11

sacred drug 53
sacred reality 76
Saku, Soyen 43
Samuels, A. 101
San Francisco Zen Center 43
SBNR *See* spiritual but not religious
Schmidt, L. 100–101, 158
Schmidt, M. 158–159
Schopenhauer, A. 43

Science and Health with Key to the Scriptures (Eddy) 35
scientific supernatural 159
Second World War 41, 43
secular critiques of SBNR 103–105
self-actualization 46, 78
self-growth/self-realization hypothesis 100
self-realization 89, 97
Selling Spirituality (Carrette and King) 98, 150–151
A Separate Reality (Castaneda) 151
Sheilaism 97, 107
Siddhartha (Hesse) 154–155
sin 59, 72–73, 94
The Sixties Spiritual Awakening: American Religion Moving from Modern to Post Modern (Ellwood) 152–153
slaves 25–26
Smith, H. 43, 54
"The Social Ethic of Religiously Unaffiliated Spirituality" (Chandler) 151
social respectability 42
social spaces 44–45
spiritual awakening 73
spiritual but not religious (SBNR) 1–2, 41, 130; the 1960s 41–45; beliefs/attitudes 67–76, 94; Big Five personality traits 82; Bill W. role in origins of 10–11; characteristics of people 80–86; combinativeness 14, 62–63; critics (*see* criticisms); early American strands of 22–27; economic conditions 20–22; factors/causes of 131–132; future growth 121–123, 135; influential spokesperson 27–32; institutional religion dominance and 18–20; metaphysical curiosity 32–39; "picking and choosing" approach to belief 95; practices (*see* practices in SBNR); psychological traits, SBNR individuals 84–85; Rotary Club article, term usage in 9–10; traditional religion's problems with 93–96
"Spiritual but not Religious: A Brief Introduction" (Fuller and Parsons) 154
Spiritual, But Not Religious: Understanding Unchurched America (Fuller) 153
spiritual consumerism 99
Spiritual Dimensions of Green Politics (Spretnak) 61
spiritual eclecticism 132
spiritual energy 4, 28–32, 50, 75, 77–80, 104
spiritual experience 8, 88, 90, 150
spiritual growth 49, 71–72, 89, 156
spiritual lesbianism 60
spiritual narcissism 96–99, 134
spiritual realities 131
spiritual thinking 104
spiritual truth 39
The Spiritual Turn (Watts) 159
spiritualism 36–37
spirituality 7–8, 16n1; being spiritual 75, 123; ecological 61; feminist 58–59; to marketable product 99; nature-centered 126; of religion 9; sustainable 123–125; unchurched 15, 29, 105, 108–109, 135, 146, 152–153
spiritually eclectic 27
spiritus 6
Spretnak, C. 61
St. Paul 6
subtle energies 38, 39, 78, 111, 139
supernatural beliefs 2
supernatural powers/forces 23

supernatural realities 15
supreme good 6
Suzuki, D. T. 43, 47
Swedenborg, E. 31
syncretism 121–122

The Teachings of Don Juan: A Yaqui Way of Knowledge (Castaneda) 25
the Theosophical Society 37
Theosophy 32, 37, 38; romanticization of the "mystic East" 39; SBNR tradition, influence on 38
Thoreau, H. D. 9, 13
Thurman, H. 99, 100
The Transcendental Club 29
Transcendentalist movement/ Transcendentalism 13–14; principles 29–32
Trine, R. W. 35
"The Triumph of the Therapeutic and Being SBNR" (Fitzpatrick and Parsons) 153
Twelve Steps and Twelve Traditions 12

unchurched spirituality 15, 29, 105, 108–109, 135, 146, 153
unhealthy narcissism 106–107
Unitarian-Universalist churches 109
unseen order 6, 121, 123, 129

The Varieties of Religious Experience (James) 8, 11, 52
Vivekananda 43
Vodou 26

Watts, A. 54
Watts, G. 159
Weber, M. 49
Western culture's gnostic tradition 41
White, C. 159
Whitman, W. 9, 47
Wilson, B. *see* Bill W.
Wilson, E. O. 118
Wink, P. 100
witchcraft 23
women: ideal woman, Catholic doctrines 57; liberation movement 56–57
Wonder: From Emotion to Spirituality (Fuller) 154
World's Parliament in Chicago 43
Wuthnow, R. 69, 96, 160

yoga 4, 39, 43, 50, 55, 63, 76, 78, 79, 134, 143, 157
Yogananda 43
Yogi, Maharishi Mahesh 44

Zen *satori* 39

For Product Safety Concerns and Information please contact our EU representative GPSR@taylorandfrancis.com
Taylor & Francis Verlag GmbH, Kaufingerstraße 24, 80331 München, Germany

www.ingramcontent.com/pod-product-compliance
Lightning Source LLC
LaVergne TN
LVHW010702110826
845149LV00014B/3194

* 9 7 8 1 0 3 2 9 9 4 5 6 7 *